BREAKING
THE DEVIL'S
CONTRACT

REV. PAUL T. CROSS

BREAKING THE DEVIL'S CONTRACT

ISBN: 978-1-7356143-4-2

Dedication

This book is dedicated to my precious family and friends. You give me the courage to continue fighting the good fight of faith! You encourage me to shine the Light of Jesus to the World. God is allowing us to help the World to successfully Break the Devil's Contract and be free from the torment and control of the Devil. We have had devastating losses in our life but we will see them in Heaven soon! I want to thank them for their encouragement and kind words. You were a blessing and you will not be forgotten! You have gotten your promotion and we look forward to ours! Rest in God's Loving Arms until we see you again!

Introduction

This book exposes how the Devil gets into our lives and wreaks havoc. You will learn how the Devil operates and how to fight against him. There are areas of your life that you have signed a contract with the enemy. This contract is referred to as the Devil's Contract. God has shown me the tactics of the enemy for over 20 years now in ministry. His tactics never change but they still work on everyone the same way. You have a contract in your life that you have made with the Devil.

Have you ever wondered why you keep sinning in a certain area of your life and you can't get free from it? Most Christians only learn about what their Pastor preaches on once a week. They don't take notes and they don't even remember the sermon. If your Pastor is not preaching on "Breaking the Devil's Contract" then you will never learn what you need to fully get free from the grip of the Devil. I promise you that after you read this book you will never forget what the Devil's Contract is or how to break it. God is challenging you today to go deeper with Him and to get free from the contract you have made with the Devil. Find out what is in the contract you have made with the Devil. Once you have broken the Devil's Contract I show you how to stay free from making another contract with the Devil.

Experience the Abundant Life Jesus promised! What an awesome thing it is to have true Joy in the Lord and to be free from the bondage of sin! I will show you that you are unstoppable in Jesus when you are doing God's Will. The enemy can't hold you back anymore once you Break the Devil's Contract! This book is a powerful weapon against the Devil that you can use to get your freedom back. This is very serious and I cannot stress to you enough that you need to break the Devil's Contract! Start reading today and Break the Devil's Contract! You are more than a conqueror in Christ Jesus! Find your true identity in Christ Jesus and walk in the Joy of the Lord! You can be free from the Devil's control over your life and have Joy! The Joy of the Lord is your strength so let's get it back now!

TABLE OF CONTENTS

CHAPTER 1

What is the Devil's Contract?

"Now the Spirit expressly says that in latter times some will depart from the faith, giving heed to deceiving spirits and doctrines of demons." 1 Timothy 4:1

The Devil's Contract is a supernatural contract that is formed between a human and the Devil. Now we know the Devil cannot be everywhere at once, so he has his demons do most of the work. The Devil's Kingdom is set up strategically with ranks of demons that do different jobs. The Contract that you have made with the Devil was actually formed between you and demons. When I use the words, Devil, enemy, evil, or demons, I am referring to the Kingdom of Satan (See Glossary). Every action an evil force takes was a direct order from their hierarchy, which is Satan. They feed you their Doctrine and lies to deceive you into believing them and signing the Contract. The Contract is made up over time and continuously added to almost daily. The Devil's Contract contains the Doctrine of Demons spoken about in the Bible (1 Timothy 4:1). The Contract you signed with demons is just as real as if you signed it with Satan because he is the one to whom the Contract is submitted.

When you saw the title of this book it is very possible that you thought about someone selling their soul to the Devil. It has been referred to as making a deal with the Devil for something that you want more than anything in the World. The Devil's Contract is quite the opposite as you will find out throughout this book. You are making a deal but it does not work out the way that you think it will. There are demonic spirits that will deceive you into thinking that you are getting one over on the Devil and God. They want you to think that you are in control. You wind up being a slave to them and their

7

desires. This turns into the worst episode of the "Twilight Zone" that you can imagine because it has eternal consequences.

The Devil is in the details, and he is very technical about those details in the Contract. A judge does not need to come in person to make you submit to the court. He will simply send an enforcer or officer to make you submit to the power of the court. You submit to the Devil's power when you sign this Contract with demons. They try to hide this fact from you so you will sign it and be loyal. The Devil's Contract is formed by agreeing to any lie contrary to God's Word. You can have a Contract that is only composed of a few lies or a whole bunch of lies. The Devil's Contract has a wide array of areas where these lies are applied to your life. The Devil's Contract is only one Contract but is compiled of all of the lies he has convinced you to believe. When Breaking the Devil's Contract, it is important to do it one area or lie at a time. So, when I refer to the Contract of Fear it is just a part of the Devil's Contract. The Devil's Contract is made up of many different smaller contracts or agreements. All of these smaller contracts are compiled to make the Devil's Contract.

The Devil's Contract is brutal and cruel, but it can be broken with God's Power. The Devil's Contract is a significant Contract that binds you to a Demonic Doctrine. This Book shows you how the Contract or deal is made with the Devil. This Contract is an agreement by both parties. The Devil is in the details, and they are critical, but unfortunately, they are hidden in the fine print. So, I am sure you are curious, what is in the Contract? You might also be wondering how long you are locked in for on the Contract? How many parts does it have? What are the hidden terms? We will get to all these questions but let us look at the contents of the Contract.

A Contract is a written or spoken agreement by both parties that is enforceable. The Contract has an exchange of value. Which makes you wonder what is valuable about it for you? The type of Contract that the Devil makes with us is called an Unconscionable Contract. An Unconscionable Contract is considered unjust by being unfairly weighted to give the advantage to one side over the other. A court usually rules and determines if a contract is unconscionable. If the court was to rule a contract to be unconscionable, it would have to be defined that no mentally able person would sign it. The second part would be that no honest person would offer it as an option. The third part would be to find that the integrity of the court is in question if enforced. Some synonyms of a contract are agreement, covenant, pact, deal, bond, accounts, engagements, pledge, or promise.

There are several parts to a contract. There has to be an offer, acceptance of the agreement, a meeting of the minds, consideration, capacity, legality, and sometimes a written document to be valid. In understanding the type of Contract, you can see what I am talking about here is a contract that should be illegal. However, this Contract is binding along with any other contracts as long as you verbally agree to it or give consent. However, if you try to fight it, bring it to the courts, and expose the language in the Contract, then it will be deemed null and void by the judge. The problem is that most people cannot afford an attorney, and they do not know how to fight it themselves. The other person enforcing the Contract makes them pay dearly with all that they have.

We must follow Biblical Doctrine and let it guide us every day. Doctrine is a belief system made up of Biblical Truth from the Scriptures that are used to guide our thoughts and actions. In the Bible, it talks about there being Doctrines of Demons. The Doctrine of Demons is an evil doctrine designed to kill, steal, and destroy you. The Devil is the Author of Confusion. He is also the god of this World. The god of this World has a job to blind you from the Truth. The Bible is Absolute Truth. It says that the Devil is a liar and the Father of Lies. The Devil does not want you to know the Truth. It is his job to confuse you and to make sure that you do not understand the Truth. Part of the problem is that we do not realize when the Devil is talking to us normally.

We hear three voices daily. The first voice is our flesh. Our voice would tell us that we are hungry, thirsty, or bored. It also will tempt us to do evil things by perverting our desires. The second voice is the Voice of God. His Voice is the most unmistakable voice to discern. His Voice is always trying to tell us to do the right thing. Sometimes His Voice will warn us on making a specific decision. His Voice will not be contrary to the Word of God. The third voice is the voice of the enemy which tries to deceive us all the time. He tells us lies and tries to confuse us. He is very selfish and evil. He wants to create division in our lives between people we love. He tempts us to sin continually.

All these voices show up in our heads as thoughts. So that means all day long, you are listening to at least three voices. Other people's voices can also be speaking to you, but this is still their flesh, God, or the Devil speaking to you through them. The Bible tells us to take every thought captive to the obedience of Jesus Christ. Starting today, you must listen to every voice that comes into your head. When you listen to these voices, you need to decide which voice is speaking to you. If it is the Voice of God, then you need to obey It. If it is the voice of the enemy, then you need to rebuke it. Tell it no, and to get out of your head. The problem is that the enemy speaks to us all day long, and we do not rebuke him or tell him no. These thoughts, which are his ideas and plans, wind up nesting in our mind. We begin to dwell on these thoughts and accept them as our new reality, which is giving consent to the Devil and forming a contract. If it's your flesh, we need to refuse it because it wants us to do evil.

Now sometimes, our thoughts can be demonic. Our thoughts can be evil. Our flesh is corrupt, and it is continually active. Our flesh wants to try to kill us. Now what I mean is that if you are at McDonald's and you have the option of anything on the menu or a salad, then you are probably going to pick the unhealthy option. Our flesh in the Bible is described as a mindset that can be temporarily trained. Our flesh will never be saved, but only our spirit can be saved. Our flesh can be trained to do good things in certain areas, but ultimately it is trying to keep us from God and is drawn toward sin. Our flesh or our sinful nature needs to be sanctified daily. That means we are at war with the flesh every day. We are at war with our flesh and the enemy, which are demons. However, we can fight the enemy with the Spirit of God that is inside of us. The Holy Spirit lives inside us once we are saved and will give us victory over our flesh. However, just like in a real war, if the soldier has a weapon in his hands, it is up to the soldier to use it to defend himself to win over the enemy. If the soldier lays down his weapon and becomes a pacifist, then the enemy will gladly accept that surrender, put them in jail for the rest of their life, and torture them the whole time with intimidation.

The Bible tells us that we are supposed to fight the good fight of faith to fight against the enemy and our flesh every day. If we do not fight daily, we will wind up being tempted by our flesh and the enemy then falling easily into that temptation. If we continue in sin, then we will be far away from God. We will not want to pray, read our Bible, or even go to Church. We will lose our desire for the things of God when we sin. It is just like going to the gym. If we go to the gym every day and workout, then we will feel great. However, if we stop going to the gym one day, then we do not want to go the next day. Before we know it, it has been several days since we have been to the gym, and we do not even miss it. That is our flesh; it wants us to go the path of least resistance no matter what it is. The Bible says we are to make no provision for the flesh

Romans 13:14, *"But put on the Lord Jesus Christ, and make no provision for the flesh, to fulfill its lusts."* In the Bible, the flesh is not our human body, but rather it is our sinful nature that lives within us that is evil and is at war against God.

As you can see, we have a war on our hands daily, and most of us have not been fighting it. God is speaking to us all day long to do the right thing, avoid the enemy, and be blessed. The enemy is talking to us trying to get us to sin. The enemy is not always trying to get us to only sin with our bodies. He wants us to be in rebellion toward God with our minds. Correct Doctrinal Theology is critical in our everyday lives. Theology is the study of God. Doctrine is the specific belief that applies to our understanding of God and His Word. Satan is continually trying to get us to abandon Bible Doctrine.

One fundamental Christian Doctrine is Absolute Truth. This means that the Word of God is the ultimate Biblical Authority of Truth. Absolute Truth cannot be disputed and is infallible. If you believe that God's Word is true, then the enemy will always try to change your mind. If you are unsure that God's Word is the Absolute Truth, then he has you already. It is his job to deceive us because he is the god of this World, and he blinds us to the Truth. The Bible says that the Devil is the Author of Confusion.

Everything the Devil says to you is a proposal. Remember that! He is constantly proposing his ideas to you in such a way that he wants to get you to agree with them. You have a choice and the Power in Jesus to disagree with him. When he presents it to you, and you do not disagree, then you are giving him consent. Therefore, the Devil talks to you all day long and reveals to you his ideas. He wants you to follow him and believe his lies. If you believe his doctrine or thoughts and accept them as your own, you create a contract between you and the Devil. You accept his proposal and agree to it. He wants you to believe a lie, and this is spiritual bullying. The Devil wants you to believe his doctrine. In doing this, he will supply you with an Unconscionable Contract. It is unfair to you and robs you of your rights. The Word of God says that Jesus Christ died for our sins, and if we believe that we go to Heaven.

The Devil wants you to believe that Jesus Christ never existed. That means He did not die for your sins, and if you believe that, then you will not go to Heaven. Therefore, since you have believed in the Devil's lies, then you have signed a contract. This Contract you signed by agreement is legally binding. This means you agreed that the Devil is telling you the truth in some area of your life. Therefore, in judgment day, when you stand before God, you will be shocked to see Jesus with scars on His Hands from being nailed to the cross for your sins. Since you did not accept Jesus as your Savior, you will be sent to hell for all eternity. It robs you of the benefits of being forgiven for your sins while on earth and going to Heaven when you die.

Truth in advertising is an organization dedicated to holding companies accountable for how they advertise to the public. The website they have is terrific at informing you of illegal marketing practices and the companies that have used them. They say, "One deceptive practice is Free-to-pay conversion plans, where you receive a good or service free (or at a nominal price) for an introductory period. Then, you get charged a boatload of money if you don't take affirmative steps to cancel the plan or return the good or service." Unethical advertising is another misrepresentation of a product. It uses subliminal messaging to fit a hidden agenda. This advertising uses deceptive ways to manipulate and convince the customer to buy a product. Companies have rules and regulations on how they market their products. The company has to tell the truth about the product, and they have to follow the FTC rules. The fine print can't be tiny, and the side effects must be listed. The speaker on a commercial cannot speak too quickly to where you cannot understand them.

Commercials are not supposed to be louder than regular programming. I remember many years ago having to turn down the T.V. as soon as the commercial came on. Companies have accountability, so the customer is not tricked into buying a product and being deceived. In 1958 The National Association of Broadcasters banned Subliminal Advertising because this was a huge problem. The Devil does not obey these rules, and neither does his demons. You are the only one who can hold them accountable, but it is only through God's Word that they can be found out to be deceptive. If you do not know God's Word or obey It, then the demons are running over you and deceiving you into buying their products which are lies and half-truths.

The Unconscionable Contract definition clearly says that the Contract is considered unjust if no mentally able person would sign it. However, that means that only a crazy person would sign a contract that robs them of being forgiven for their sins and going to Heaven for all eternity. So, it seems only a crazy person would believe the lies of Satan, right? No, we all have been deceived by Satan. Therefore, a court would look at this Contract that you signed and consider it Unconscionable, and the Contract would be thrown out. However, the only way this would happen is if you tried to dispute it. Once most people have agreed to something, they will blindly hold onto a lie. Do not let your pride stop you from believing God's Word.

Yelp is a go-to resource currently for getting reviews on a business. Instead of risking going to a place with bad service or getting a bad deal for your money, most people will do the research and go on yelp. They will look carefully at the reviews and decide whether they believe that person is giving their honest opinion. Then they will determine whether they should go and visit that business. So, people do research just for the simple task of getting something to eat for a meal. However, when it comes to hearing voices in your head, people will just silently allow that voice to take over and convince them of some weird thing that is a lie. The enemy will tell you that it is ok to stay home and watch the football game instead of going to Church. The enemy will tell you to stay at home and not go to Church because it is your only day off. Before you know it, you do not go to Church anymore. You look back, and it has been over five years since you went to Church. How did this happen?

The Bible says to take our thoughts captive to the obedience of Christ. If we do not use God's Word as a filter for our thoughts, then we will be gullible and believe any lie the enemy tells us. He loves to tell Christians that, "Church doesn't matter" and "It's ok if you don't go to Church, God will forgive you." Therefore, when the enemy tells you these lies, you just go with it. The Bible says that we are supposed to fight the good fight of faith. The Christian life is a fight and a daily battle. However, it is not always just a war. If you follow God and have an intimate relationship with Him daily, your life will be filled with unspeakable Joy. The Bible says in Nehemiah 8:10, "The Joy of the Lord is our strength." Joy is a supernatural Gift that only the Lord gives. Galatians 5:22-23 says, "The fruit of the Spirit is Love, Joy, Peace, Patience, Goodness, Gentleness, faithfulness, meekness, and self-control." The Fruit of the Spirit occurs as we spend time with the Lord. The Fruit of Joy will fill our hearts, and it is a supernatural overflow of the Holy Spirit inside of us. Spending time with God and doing His Will allows us to experience the Joy of the Lord.

We have to take our thoughts captive, or we will be held captive! Silent consent happens when the Devil talks to us about the Bible, sin, or about Christian Doctrine, and we just agree with him out of fear or another reason. The Devil is a bully. He wants to threaten us and scare us to believe "His truth." We think that if we just agree with the Devil, he will leave us alone. This is a massive lie that he wants us to believe. If we agree with the Devil, then this gives him a right to oppress us from here on out. We sign a contract that gives him the right to come into our minds permanently. This is like inviting an evil vampire to come into your house. According to most movies, once you do this, they can go inside from now on because you gave them permission once. You may not want them to go into your house every day, but you gave them a key to every lock in your home. Therefore, you are never safe from the enemy. We do this when we agree with Satan and his Doctrine of Demons and sign the Devil's Contract. Demonic Doctrine becomes a satanic stronghold in your mind, and the enemy will not give up his access point or key because you gave him a legal right to be there. The enemy builds a fortress in your mind (Demonic Stronghold) and fights against God.

The enemy is continually talking to you. You are probably being talked to right now, and the enemy is trying to distract you from reading the rest of this chapter or reading the rest of this book. He knows that you will break the Contract that you made with him, and he hates that. However, you must choose to be free and break the Devil's Contract. The most important lie that he can ever tell anyone is that he does not exist or that Jesus is not Lord. If you have believed either one of those lies, then you have signed a Contract of Unbelief. To break the Devil's Contract, you must accept Jesus Christ as your Lord. This book is about exposing the lies of the enemy and giving your life to Jesus. You need the Power of God to break the Devil's Contract, and only Jesus has it.

Jesus was prophesied as the coming Messiah to forgive people of their sins. He was to be born of a virgin, of the royal lineage of David, sinless, God in the flesh, crucified, and raised from the dead. Jesus accomplished all of the things prophesied about Him. He lived a sinless life and was crucified on the cross for the sin of all humanity. The Bible says in John 3:16, *"God so loved the world that He gave His only begotten Son, whoever believes in Him will not perish but have everlasting life."* Jesus is the Son of God. He died for humanity, and salvation is provided as a gift. In the Old Testament, an animal's blood was shed as an offering or atonement for sin. This was a prophecy and foreshadowed what Jesus would do for all of humanity to appease the blood atonement for sin. Jesus is the Lamb of God who takes away the sin of the World (John 1:29).

Jesus had dominion over Satan as He walked the earth to the amazement of everyone that saw it at that time. He healed the sick and cast out demons. He was the only one to ever do this until this time. He was not a magician because none of the magicians could replicate His miracles. He was the Son of God recorded in history. He was here. He died on the cross, rose again on the third day, and was seen by many people. He went to Heaven and sent the Holy Spirit to come into the hearts of all believers. Anyone who believes in Jesus as their Savior will be forgiven of their sins and receive salvation.

Jesus is real, and He wants to save you from the enemy and from your flesh that is trying to kill you and send you to hell for all eternity. To receive Jesus, you must believe that He is the Son of God and that He died on the cross for your sins. You must accept His atonement for your sins. You must acknowledge that you are a sinner that needs a Savior. God is a Holy God that will not allow anyone to get into Heaven because of sin. He has judged sin through Jesus Christ's sacrificial death on the cross. However, for you to escape the Wrath of God, you must accept Jesus. God poured out His wrath on Jesus for sin on the cross. Jesus said to the Father in Matthew 27:46, "*My God, My God, why have You forsaken Me?*" He felt the judgment of sin rest on Him as He hung on the cross. He became our sin offering. There is no other way to be saved from hell and be judged by God except through Jesus Christ.

If you acknowledge this as the Truth, then you need to accept it as Absolute Truth. Whatever lies the Devil has told you about Jesus or salvation needs to be broken. Salvation is a free gift that cannot be earned. You must accept it and not try to add on to it by believing any of the lies the Devil has told you about salvation. Jesus alone is Salvation. You must confess and repent from your sins by grace through faith. Grace means it cannot be earned, and it is only through faith and acceptance of Jesus and what He did on the cross. If you have never accepted Jesus as your Savior, then you are at a crossroad. The Lord had you read this book to find out that God loves you and sent His Son Jesus to die on the cross and forgive you of your sins. God wants you to accept His Gift so your sins will be forgiven, and you will have a right relationship with God restored. You will be forgiven and free.

God loves you and sent His Son Jesus to be your Savior. He died for you and will forgive you for anything you have ever done in your life. Yes, anything, no matter what! This is an Absolute Truth. John 14:6 says, "*Jesus said to him, I am the way, the truth, and the life. No one comes to the Father except through Me.*" Jesus is telling us that He is the only way to be saved and have forgiveness of sins. God will accept you once you accept Him. John 3:16 says, "*For God so loved the world that He gave His only begotten Son, that whoever believes in Him should not perish but have everlasting life.*" So if you believe Jesus is the Son of God then you will be saved and forgiven. You must repent of your sins and accept Jesus as your Savior. The Devil has deceived you into thinking that you do not need Jesus. You can feel the tug on your heart of the Holy Spirit right now. This is proof that God is real. He is reaching out to you to help you to break the lies of the enemy to find Him. He is the Way, the Truth, and the Life.

If you are ready to accept Jesus as your Savior, then repeat this prayer with all of your heart. "God, I believe that I am a sinner, and I need forgiveness. I cannot save myself and I accept the sacrifice that Jesus provided on the cross for my sin. I repent of my sins and believe that Jesus is the Son of God. Lord, please forgive me for all of my sins. I make you Lord of my life. Thank you for forgiving me of my sin. Wipe my slate clean and help me to serve you. In Jesus Name, I pray Amen." If you prayed this prayer for the first time, then the Holy Spirit has come into your heart, and you are saved.

You have a relationship with God, and you are forgiven. You have felt your sin lift off of you, and your heart became clean and renewed. You are a born-again Child of God. All of Heaven is rejoicing with you as you have made Jesus the Lord of your life. The journey is just beginning, and God will show you His Love and Power as you walk closely with Him all the days of your life. God will never leave you or forsake you. You do have an enemy, but the Lord Jesus has given you the Power to fight him and win. Rejoice and be glad for great is your reward in Heaven. Keep reading in this book for Biblical Wisdom that will help you to become a disciple and have a close relationship to the Lord while winning the fight against the enemy.

If you prayed this prayer and nothing happened, then one of two things occurred. First, you have prayed this prayer before, and you are already saved. Now, for the people reading this book thinking you will shortcut the process and just learn knowledge, it will not help you get saved. The second is that you did not fully believe or think you are ready to commit your life to Jesus. This is sad because you are not promised tomorrow. You may not ever get another chance to get saved. The death rate for humanity is 100 percent. You will die, but the Devil wants to tell you that you will get a chance on your deathbed. However, very few people are awake on their deathbeds. They die instantly in their sleep or in a coma where they get unplugged later by a loved one. You are not promised tomorrow and God is giving you this chance. Today is the day of salvation. Choose this day who you will serve.

God is a gentleman, and He will not force His way into your life. He wants you to choose Him. He gives you the freedom to choose, but the consequences are eternal death and hell if you make the wrong choice. He wants you to lay down your pride and plans for your life and choose Him. God has the best plan in store for your life, and He is Amazing. I lived a life full of sin before being saved. It appears to be fun but leads to a life of guilt, shame, and emptiness. Pray the prayer if you want to know God right now. If you pray this prayer with all of your heart, then Jesus will show you that He is real.

Jesus said in Revelations 3:20, *"Behold, I stand at the door and knock. If anyone hears My voice and opens the door, I will come into him and dine with him, and he with Me."* No matter what you have done, God will forgive you of your sins if you ask Him. Pray this prayer and see how far down the rabbit hole goes. "God, I have lived my life, and it is empty. I know that something is missing. I am a sinner, and I need forgiveness. I am sorry for my sin, and I accept Jesus as my Savior, I am sorry for doubting You, I accept You today. Show Yourself real to me. Come into my heart and forgive me of my sin. I repent of my sins and I make You Lord of my life. Save me and help me to serve You. I allow You full access to my heart and life. I need You. Thank You for forgiving me of my sins. I want a real relationship with You. In Jesus Name, I pray. Amen."

We have an enemy, and he has deceived us in many ways. This book will explore all the ways that you may have entered into a contract with him during your life. This book is filled with the Word of God because only It will set you free. The next chapter is the foundation for the Devil's Contract. Do not allow the enemy to stop you from reading the rest of this book. God has brought you to this book but you do not fully understand what the Devil's Contract is or how it is formed. You need to learn about all of the different areas of the Devil's Contract and especially how to break it. God will remind you to finish this book. God led you to this book so keep reading and break the Devil's Contract over your life! Learn how to be free in Jesus and to have Joy again! Restore the Joy of your salvation! Just trying to survive each day is not the Abundant Life that Jesus died for you to have! Keep reading and I promise you will be able to have the Holy Spirit in your life in such a way that you will be full of Joy until it bursts out of you! Don't put God in a box.

CHAPTER 2

Absolute Truth

"Sanctify them by Your truth. Your word is truth." John 17:17

The Bible is clear that it is the Word of God. It was written by 40 authors and has 66 books. As we discussed in the previous chapter, it is vital to establish Absolute Truth. One Absolute Truth is that humans live on earth. The Sun gives light to our Planet is another Absolute Truth. These are agreed upon by all people living on earth. Now in saying that, there are people that would dispute these two claims just to be debating them. That does not mean they have a case or that they are right. However, they want their voice to be heard. In arguing their case, it could create a whole group of followers and even a Religion with millions of people. People will fall for anything because they do not have any Biblical Absolute Truth that grounds them. You have heard the saying, "That if you do not stand for something, you will fall for anything." I really like that saying. It proves the point that we as Christians need to stand for the Word of God and do not waiver from any words that are recorded inside of It.

The Word of God is vital to the life of the Christian. To be upfront, I want to clarify the definition I will be using in this book for Religion (See Glossary). When I use the word Religion, I am speaking of a man-made organization composed of human ideas and theologies that are not always Biblical. Religion is, therefore, faulty and not an Absolute Truth. There is no one Religion (Man-made) that is perfect or without flaws. In saying that, I would identify as a Christian (Acts 11:26) but have to say I do not agree with every Doctrine, sect, or Church that labels itself as Christian. I declare myself a Non-Denominational

Christian. This means that I do not cling to anyone's denomination inside of Christianity. Non-Denominational goes back to the Bible's original intent in identifying Christians as followers of Jesus and the correct interpretation of the Bible in practicing everything that the Bible teaches. The definition of Christianity confuses most people. Christianity seems to allow homosexual priests. It seems to allow any Pastor to avoid topics like sin, hell, and the crucifixion. Christianity is a word that is loaded with misconceptions and misunderstandings.

The Bible says that we must believe on the Lord for salvation as the Blood sacrifice for our sins. We must confess Jesus before men or Jesus will not confess us before the Father (Matthew 10:33). There are many Scriptures about confessing Jesus to be saved to go to Heaven alone, but I find that if you present the Gospel to someone and lead them in a prayer affirming their beliefs, there is a confirmation by God that is noticeable by the person praying. However, you may not have said a prayer like this one when you got saved, but you only said Jesus forgive me, I believe in You, help me. This confirms your belief in Jesus, and if you felt God forgive you and fill your heart, then you are saved. Now it is crucial that you continue, get baptized, and serve the Lord.

The Scriptures are the Word of God. 2 Timothy 3:14-17 says,

"But you must continue in the things which you have learned and been assured of, knowing from whom you have learned them, and that from childhood you have known the Holy Scriptures, which are able to make you wise for salvation through faith which is in Christ Jesus. All Scripture is given by inspiration of God, and is profitable for doctrine, for reproof, for correction, for instruction in righteousness, that the man of God may be complete, thoroughly equipped for every good work."

The Bible is called the Holy Scriptures, according to Paul. He says that all Scripture is inspired by God and used for Doctrine. Doctrine is a set of beliefs guided by the interpretation of the Scriptures. We see a few significant truths here about the Scriptures in just this one passage. The Scriptures are Holy, inspired by God, and used for Doctrine. The Scriptures are the Word of God. The Word of God is Absolute Truth since God cannot lie. Titus 1:1-2 says,

"Paul, a bondservant of God and an apostle of Jesus Christ, according to the faith of God's elect and the acknowledgment of the truth which accords with godliness, in hope of eternal life which God, who cannot lie, promised before time began."

God is not a liar, but Satan is verified as the father of all lies. John 8:44 says,

"You are of your father, the devil, and the desires of your father you want to do. He was a murderer from the beginning and does not stand in the truth, because there is no truth in him. When he speaks a lie, he speaks from his own resources, for he is a liar and the father of it."

Jesus is speaking about Satan, and Jesus cannot lie, so Satan is a liar. Amen!

Since we agree that God is not a liar, then it is easy to make the Word of God the Absolute authority in our lives. Humanity has made unlimited attempts at creating new Religions, all with their own theologies and doctrines that are not Bible-based. The Bible says that the Word of God is inspired by God. That means it is written by man but under the influence of the Holy Spirit. So, men allowed God to use them to write under the inspiration of the Holy Spirit. God dictated what He wanted them to write about, and they listened to His Voice and wrote down the Scriptures. This is how it happened in layman's terms. The Bible says all Scripture is inspired by God (2 Timothy 3:16). All in the Greek original language in the Bible means all! So when the Devil tries to lie and tell you that certain parts of the Bible are just man's opinion or whatever lies he tells you, then you can use this Scripture as Absolute Truth to prove the Devil or anyone else wrong. Yes, they can argue all day long and try to give you arguments that seem to have some type of half-truths involved, but we know the Truth at the end of the day. He says that all Scripture is Inspired and used as Doctrine. Doctrines are the building blocks of the Christian Faith.

Half-truths are very powerful. We get confused by half-truths when arguing. That is because there is a deception mixed in with the truth. Our minds want to accept the true part, and we sometimes ignore the lie. Since there is some truth, then we tend to believe the whole statement. This is where the fact-checking is so essential these days. You hear someone ramble off a list of so called facts, and then because they are well respected we believe they are telling the truth and we accept it as such. Then we find out later that they were not quoting the correct facts. They were lying or giving half-truths. Here is a half-truth; "Jesus is a prophet but not the Messiah." This is what a popular Religion teaches. If we agree with them, then the whole Bible falls apart. This is a lie that has a partial truth to it. Jesus was a Prophet, and that is because He knows the future. However, He was God and the Messiah or the Savior in the flesh. If we agree with the half-truth, then we deny Jesus as Savior, and Jesus becomes a dead Prophet in a tomb somewhere. The Devil has many people deceived because he has tried to dilute the Word of God and his lies have been forced down our throats. These are the Doctrine of Demons that the Bible mentions. Half-truths are lies that must be disputed with the Word of God.

The Bible is referred to as a mirror. It shows us what our actual condition looks like. It helps us to see what is wrong with us. The Bible is also a scale. If you are trying to lose weight, it is important to weigh yourself to see where you are. If you are 250 lbs. and your goal weight is 200 lbs, you will make sure to use your scale as a part of the weight loss program. It helps to see if you have made any progress or if you are gaining weight. We don't get mad at the scale if it shows us that we are gaining weight, do we? That would be absurd. Now people do this kind of stuff all of the time. However, it is unfruitful.

So, picture this, you have worked out all week and hit the gym hard. Your current weight is 250 lbs as of Monday, and you feel that you have done enough working out to have lost at least 5 lbs. It is now one week later, and you are ready to weigh yourself. You get on the scale, and it reads 250 lbs. You think to yourself this scale must be wrong. However, you test it out every day by putting a 20 lb. weight on it to make sure it is accurate and reads 20 lbs. Therefore, you know that it is telling the truth. No matter what your feelings are telling you, the scale is correct. However, you know for sure that you should have lost weight. Then you remember that you didn't change your diet at all. You feel like a fool, but you were eating buffets for dinner every day.

See, the Word of God is like a scale. It will tell you the Truth no matter what you think. It reveals the Truth to us at all times. Unlike the scale, the Word of God can never be off. Someone could comment and say that you look like you have lost weight, and you can believe it, but when you step on the scale, you will find out the truth. This is how the Word of God operates. We may feel a certain way about a sinful activity or Doctrine, but you have to be ready to accept the Truth when you open the pages and read, just as when you step on a scale. It's time to repent from your opinions and believe the Word of God.

The Reformers during the Reformation Period had a problem with the Church using the Word of God for their corrupt purposes. This is the opposite of what should have happened. The Reformers saw the Church was abusing their authority while disrespecting the Word of God. The term "Sola Scriptura" (Scripture Alone) was popularized and preached during this time. It was a sign that Christians would no longer allow Religion to be in control. They submitted to the Word of God as the Absolute Authority in the World. The corrupt Church was abusing its power as it does in many ways today. The many Religions and Churches of today will all answer for the Doctrine they are preaching and forcing on people. We are to submit to what the Word of God says and follow It fully. We are not to submit to a Religion or a Pastor blindly without doing our research.

Believing in the Word of God as Absolute Truth is the cornerstone of the Christian Faith. We must believe and fight to our last breath to preserve the integrity of the Word of God. Remember the saying, "If you do not stand for something, you will fall for anything." Many Religions teach things similar to Christianity and even call themselves Christians, but they are not. Think about why other religions that are totally different from Christianity still call themselves Christians. The Devil wants us to believe and follow his false replica so we are deceived from believing the real Truth. It is a fake Religion just like a knockoff of an original product. We must not accept a fake when our eternal life depends on it. We must be diligent in reading the Word of God, so we know It for ourselves. It is impossible to know the Word of God for yourself if you do not study It. I know many people that have not read the whole Bible, and this is a shame. The Bible says that it is our responsibility to handle the Word of Truth correctly and know It. 2 Timothy 2:15-17 says,

"Be diligent to present yourself approved to God, a worker who does not need to be ashamed, rightly dividing the word of truth. However, shun profane and idle babblings, for they will increase to more ungodliness. And their message will spread like cancer."

We must be diligent with reading the Word of God, which is pleasing to God. It says a worker that does not need to be ashamed. The enemy puts us to shame when we do not know God's Word, and the Devil takes advantage of us when this happens. We are to study and rightly divide and understand the

Word of Truth. In addition, we are to shun or shut down profane and idle babblings. We are supposed to speak up and shut down the lies of the enemy! He calls us workers. It is our job.

These babblings will increase to more ungodliness, and their message will spread like cancer (vs. 17). It is amazing and, on purpose, that he uses the word cancer. Cancer is something that does not do you in right away. It eats at you until you are weak and powerless. It can take over your whole body and kill you. This Scripture gives an insight into how the Devil operates. We have a job to do, and it all starts with us agreeing that the Word of God is the Absolute Truth. We must auto correct every time we hear someone saying something contrary to the Word of God. This means that we have an obligation from God to read His Word. We can easily dispute something that someone is saying if we know the Truth. This could lead them from an eternity in hell to being with us in Heaven, all because you obeyed God and read the Scriptures. You could say a prayer with them and lead them to God. They could become a Christian because of you. We have to set our thought filter to auto correct every lie we hear from others or the enemy. Take every thought captive to the obedience of Christ Jesus. Hold up the idea or thought to the Word of God, and if it doesn't match then it is trash and we know where trash goes!

We are going to pray and Break the Devil's Contract right now. Yes, we are praying again. It is as essential as breathing oxygen, so get used to it! We are going to pray to renounce Satan's lies that we have believed about the Word of God. This is important to do because if we do not, then Satan still has an open door. He has access to our life, and his words are like a cancer. The lies he has been telling us eat at us until it we are consumed by them. Take a second and ask God to show you in what area you have been deceived about the Word of God. Ask Him to show you what lie you have believed in making the Word of God just another book. Maybe you have disrespected the Word of God at one point and threw Bibles away or disagreed with certain parts because you didn't understand It. Perhaps you are mad at God right now and don't want to hear His Voice in written form. There are many reasons why someone does not want to agree with the Word of God as Absolute Truth. We have to realize that we may think our way is best, but we can be off. In London, everyone checks their wristwatch according to Big Ben. Your watch can say it is Noon, but if Big Ben disagrees, then you have to reset your watch!

Satan has told many lies about the Word of God. His lies need to be exposed, and the Truth needs to be elevated over the lies you were told or even your own feelings. Maybe you thought that the Word of God is outdated. Perhaps you believed the Word of God was translated wrong. Whatever lies you have been told by the enemy are demonic. I could sit here and show you the error of all of these lies, but it would take up volumes of books to do that. The Devil tells new lies every day. Hebrews 4:12-13 says,

"For the word of God is living and powerful, and sharper than any two-edged sword, piercing even to the division of soul and spirit, and of joints and marrow, and is a discerner of the thoughts and intents of the heart. And there is no creature hidden from His sight, but all things are naked and open to the eyes of Him to whom we must give account."

The Word of God is powerful, and It pierces our hearts and divides our thoughts and intents of the heart. The Lord knows what part of His Word offends you, and you must make a decision to repent. You are wrong if you have any opinion other than that of the Holy Scriptures. The Word of God is true, and every man is a liar. We must submit to the Authority of the Scriptures, which are the Word of God. Today you must choose. Draw a line in the sand. Decide to believe the Word of God over the lies of the enemy. Let's pray to break the contract with the Devil. The enemy had us believe that God's Word is not the Absolute Truth, and we must renounce that lie. Let's pray for forgiveness for not obeying the Word, reject the lies, and believe the Truth.

Let's pray, repeat these words out loud, and pray with sincerity and all of your heart. "Lord, I come to you as a sinner. I am sorry that I have mistreated Your Word. Forgive me for believing a lie over Your Word. I renounce the lies of Satan about Your Word. I believe that Your Word is the Absolute Truth. I believe that You cannot lie, and You would not lie to me. Lord, help me to accept Your Truth as my new truth. Help me to defend It. Help me to understand It. Forgive me and help me to obey the Scriptures in the future. I break the Contract of Doubt the enemy has had me believe. I receive your forgiveness Lord and I agree with Your Truth. In Jesus Name, I pray. Amen." Let's continue on to break the Devil's Contract into a million pieces!

CHAPTER 3

The Contract of Deception

"So, the great dragon was cast out, that serpent of old, called the Devil and Satan, who deceives the whole world; he was cast to the earth, and his angels were cast out with him." Revelations 12:9

The Devil is known for his deception. The Devil tries to trick people into believing certain things about the Bible. If he can, he will try to deceive you into joining a Religion that doesn't have Jesus at all. He is continuously keeping people busy with idle chat and gossip about the new normal. But as with the virus, the Devil tries to get you to accept a new reality. A reality that is normal for him but new and strange to you. Adam and Eve experienced a new normal, and it was all brought on by the Devil. Genesis 3:13 says, "And the Lord God said to the woman, "What is this you have done?" The woman said, "The serpent deceived me, and I ate." So, we can see here the Devil intended to deceive Eve. He set out to deceive Eve. This shows us the tactic of how Satan operates. Satan is a liar and a deceiver. He is not to be listened to or trusted for any reason.

God is not the author of confusion, and He wants you to know the Truth and not be deceived. The Devil does not want you to see the Truth. The Bible says the Truth will set you free. The Devil, when he approached Eve, did not tell her that he wanted to deceive her. He kept his motives hidden. He did not want the truth to get out about his intentions. The Devil operates the same way today. The Devil seeks to deceive the whole World. He has been doing it since the time of Adam and Eve and is very good at it. He deceived Eve, and she didn't have a fallen, sinful nature. She was pure and had never sinned before.

The Bible says that the Devil appears as an Angel of Light. Satan is smooth as silk, and we have to be on guard now that we know how he operates as a deceiver. Our light in the darkness is the Word of God Psalms 119:105, "Thy word is a lamp unto my feet, and a light unto my path." We need the Word of God as our light in this World. It illuminates our path to see the right way to go. If we ignore God's Word, then we will wind up in darkness. Let's look at what happened to Adam and Eve. Genesis 2:16-17 says,

"And the Lord God commanded the man, saying, "Of every tree of the garden you may freely eat; but of the tree of the knowledge of good and evil you shall not eat, for in the day that you eat of it you shall surely die."

It's clear that God spoke to Adam here, directly telling him that he is not to eat of the tree of the knowledge of good and evil. He says that the day you eat of it, you SHALL SURELY DIE. God was warning Adam. Now, Eve is made from the rib of Adam, and it was told to Eve that she is not to eat of the tree Genesis 3:1-5 says,

"Now the serpent was the most cunning of all the wild animals that the Lord God had made. He said to the woman, "Did God really say, you can't eat from any tree in the garden?" The woman said to the serpent, "We may eat the fruit from the trees in the garden. But about the fruit of the tree in the middle of the garden, God said, you must not eat it or touch it, or you will die." "No! You will certainly not die," the serpent said to the woman. "In fact, God knows that when you eat it, your eyes will be opened, and you will be like God, knowing good and evil."

The Devil has specific schemes that he uses to get you to disobey God and sin. The way that he does it is very evident in this passage, let's look a little closer. In verse 1, the Devil is already twisting the Word of God to deceive Eve. He said paraphrasing, "Did God say you can't eat any fruit at all?" Eve replied and said, yeah, all the fruit except the tree in the middle of the garden if we eat or touch that we will die. Satan, immediately with boldness, said, "No, you will certainly not die." So, we see the first bald-faced lie recorded in Scripture. He calls God a liar. Eve I'm sure is wondering just what is going on. Her God is being called a liar! Satan continues to say, "God knows that when you eat it, your eyes will be opened, and you will be like God, knowing good and evil."

The Devil tricked them with half-truths, which are powerful. A good liar uses half-truths so that it is believable. The half-truth is that their eyes would be opened but would have to disobey God and sin to do it. Satan says God is hiding a secret from them. They could eat and be like God, so they would be enlightened or know good and evil. Satan presented this to Eve as if God was holding something good back from Adam and Eve. Satan deceives them to believe that God is the bad guy in this scenario. So not only has Satan called God a liar, but he has lied to Eve, spoken half-truths, deceived her, and made her feel that God was withholding something good from her that she needed. The rest of the story unfolds here Genesis 3:6-7,

"So, when the woman saw that the tree was good for food, that it was pleasant to the eyes, and a tree desirable to make one wise, she took of its fruit and ate. She also gave to her husband with her, and he ate. Then the eyes of both of them were opened, and they knew that they were naked; and they sewed fig leaves together and made themselves coverings."

Eve does some fact-checking with her eyes. Now we know a reason why the Bible says that we walk by faith and not by sight! But Eve here is way past that point because she has been deceived and is ready to sin. She saw it was good for food, a delight to look at, and desirable for obtaining wisdom. Since she saw what the Devil was telling her had checked out to be accurate according to her reasoning, then she ate. So, she fact-checked the Devil with her eyes and mind then justified the lie and went with it. She did not go back, and fact check what the Devil was saying with the Word of God that she HAD MEMORIZED! She quoted the Word of God to the Devil but did not trust the Word of God. She repeated the Word of God the way that Satan wanted her to, so the deception would sink in further.

So, Eve fact-checked the Devil based on her logic and sight. She did not use what God had warned her about, which is His Word. God is not all about rules to make our lives miserable. He loves us and wants to protect us from the enemy and ourselves. But we have to be careful not to fact-check the Devil with our feelings and emotions. "I see that this looks good and I bet it would make me feel good, so I will do it on a whim." Eve did not take long to make up her mind.

She did not contemplate her disobedience for long. This is Eve's fault, but the Devil is powerful and skilled at lying, manipulation, and deception. We have an enemy that wants to kill, steal, and destroy our lives, according to John 10:10.

We cannot fact check the Devil in our own wisdom. We have to bring those thoughts and lies to the obedience of Christ and hold them captive or see if they line up with what God said about the subject. If they do not line up, then we are to rebuke those lies and the one who is talking to us with the Word of God. The Devil twisted the Word of God, with Jesus in the wilderness. Matthew 4:1-4 says,

"Then Jesus was led by the Spirit into the wilderness to be tempted by the devil. After fasting forty days and forty nights, he was hungry. The tempter came to him and said, "If you are the Son of God, tell these stones to become bread." Jesus answered, "It is written: Man shall not live on bread alone, but on every word that comes from the mouth of God."

Jesus was led by God into the wilderness to be tempted by the Devil. Since Adam and Eve's time, Satan has had thousands of years of experience lying, manipulating, and deceiving people. So, he faced Jesus with strategic confidence. The first thing he said to Jesus was an attack on his human ego, deity, emotions, and human needs, all while daring Him to sin. Jesus replied saying, "Man shall not live on bread alone, but on every word that comes from the mouth of God." Jesus did not fall into the trap of saying I am the Son of God, and I can prove it right now! I'm going to turn these stones to bread to show you! Jesus was confident in who He was and His mission. If He allowed His Ego to get bruised or His Emotions to get in the way, then He would have lost the battle of temptation against the Devil. Jesus would have misused the Power of God for His selfish reasons only to eat. The Devil also was trying to get Him to end the fast by sinning. Wow!

Jesus was in warfare, but He knew how to fight the Devil correctly. Jesus used the Word of God against Satan. Jesus did not fact check Satan with His eyes or emotions. He used the Sword of the Spirit against Satan. He fought back using the Word, "It is written: 'Man shall not live on bread alone, but on every word that comes from the mouth of God." Jesus ignored all of Satan's attempts to deceive Him, and He used the Word to let him know that bread is not important enough for Him to misuse the Power of God. His hunger can wait.

He said that the Word of God is the Bread that sustains Him. Jesus was quoting Deuteronomy 8:3 here to Satan,

> *"So He humbled you, allowed you to hunger, and fed you with manna which you did not know nor did your fathers know, that He might make you know that man shall not live by bread alone, but man lives by every Word that proceeds from the mouth of the Lord."*

The battle continues in Matthew 4:5-6 when the Devil tempts Jesus,

> *"Then the devil took him to the holy city and had him stand on the highest point of the temple. "If you are the Son of God," he said, "throw yourself down. For it is written: "He will command his angels concerning you, and they will lift you up in their hands, so that you will not strike your foot against a stone."*

Jesus was confronted again to prove He was the Son of God by misusing the Power of God. Just a side note here, but since Satan knows the Word of God and has it memorized and you don't, then how will you know the Truth and not be deceived? We have to read the Word of God not out of obligation but to survive an attack from the enemy. If you don't have any bullets in your gun, then the enemy is going to win. But when you choose to follow God, He will train you on how to get close to Him and understand His Word and fight the enemy. The Christian life is a marathon and not a sprint. Jesus is excellent and shows us exactly how to fight Satan. We must learn from this encounter so we can fight the enemy the same way.

Now we see that Jesus was fasting, so He was submitted to God. James 4:7 says, "Submit to God, resist the Devil, and he will flee from you." We must submit to God, walk with Him, read His Word, pray, be filled with the Spirit, then resist the Devil, and he will flee. We must have the Power of God to resist the enemy and not just our human will. You can't just pray for 2 or 3 minutes a day casually and then think you have power over Satan. You have to be serious about your walk with God for Satan to take you seriously. Demons are well aware of the Christians that walk with God and are serious in fighting the enemy. They also know the people that do not have authority over them and do not believe. Acts 19:13-16 says,

"Then some of the itinerant Jewish exorcists took it upon themselves to call the name of the Lord Jesus over those who had evil spirits, saying, "We exorcise you by the Jesus whom Paul preaches. "Also there were seven sons of Sceva, a Jewish chief priest, who did so. And the evil spirit answered and said, "Jesus I know, and Paul I know; but who are you?" Then the man in whom the evil spirit was leaped on them, overpowered them, and prevailed against them, so that they fled out of that house naked and wounded."

The demons knew about Jesus and Paul but didn't know these imposters, so they punished them severely. Jesus said to Believers that if you have faith without doubting, you will move mountains, and the enemy cannot overpower faith-filled Christians.

The way the Devil deceives people is almost similar to something called the yes ladder. It is a sales term. The yes ladder has psychology behind it to make people want to say yes. Therefore, a salesperson will ask you, "Is your name, John?" You reply, "Yes." They say, "Do you want to save money?" You answer, "Yes." They ask, "Are you sick of overpaying?" You answer, "Yes." They ask "Are you wanting a good deal for the money you are spending on life insurance?" You reply, "Yes." They say, "Do you want the best deal I can get for you?" You respond, "Yes." They say, "Is your family more important than money?" You reply, "Yes." Then they say, "Well, for 50 dollars a month I can get you life insurance, are you ready to sign today?" You answer, "Yes." You were on a yes ladder the whole time being trained to say yes.

Salespeople know that if they call you and ask you directly if you want life insurance for 50 dollars a month, then most people will tell them no and then hang up. People have other things to spend their money on these days. But salespeople have tactics. I am not saying that salespeople are evil, but they use proven strategies that overcome people's objections to manipulate them into saying yes. Then they have buyer's remorse, but it is too late. The Devil does the same thing to us. He uses tactics to deceive us, and we need to make sure that we understand them. We cannot afford to be deceived today. If we accept one little lie, then we can eventually wind up abandoning the Christian faith.

The Devil would ask you, "Does God love you?" You reply, "Yes." Does God love everybody? You answer, "Yes." Does God want everyone to go to Heaven? You reply, "Yes." He says God is in control, right? You reply, "Yes." He says then nothing can stop God, right? You answer, "Yes." All Religions point to God, so every Religion is acceptable, right? You reply, "Yes." Then everyone will be in Heaven! But this is not true. What we don't realize is that demonic forces talk to us all the time. We hear a voice in our head, and we think it's nothing. Maybe it's our own voice, so we either ignore it, or we indulge it. We get on a train of thought like the yes ladder and have a conversation with ourselves, we think. But we are communicating with demons telling us half-truths. Half-Truths are lies. Adam and Eve were talking face to face with the Devil. Jesus also spoke face to face with Satan. These days we do not talk face to face with demons. We don't talk face to face with God either. It is mostly in our minds and thoughts that we are communicating with supernatural beings. But they are near us and we can't see them. The same is true about God. He is Omnipresent so He is always near us and His Spirit lives within us.

Demons invade our minds by planting thoughts or temptations. It seems subtle, but it is very deliberate. The meaning of subtle is, "So delicate or precise as to be difficult to analyze or describe." The enemy is speaking to us delicately, and it is difficult to analyze or describe. Therefore, we see here that the Devil is using a tactic to talk with us. He is not like the salesman that announces, "HEY, I'M CALLING TO SELL YOU SOMETHING AND HERE IS HOW MUCH IT COSTS PLEASE DON'T HANG UP!" No, the Devil is subtle and uses tactics. He will gently try to persuade you in such a way that it is delicate or with a soft nudge. Once you get used to identifying that voice, you realize that the subtle way he speaks is like an evil whisper that is trying to take over your mind and body if you obey it.

He will try to talk to you and confuse you on every topic imaginable. He will try to get you to waste your time with many things in this World. Look Squirrel! Just like that, the Devil will steal your attention from God, and he doesn't care as long as you just don't think about God or do anything to get closer to God. Once we get our focus off God it is hard to refocus on God because we are distracted with other activities that are enjoyable and make us feel productive. After a while, we realize that any actions we are doing are empty and we want to turn to God again to repent.

He has many deceptions that he wants you to believe. The major thing is not giving your life to Jesus and getting saved or born again. He will distract you with all of these logical questions that try to disprove God, but if that fails, then he can't stop you from getting saved. Once you get saved, then you are still a target for the enemy. He tries to get you to get distracted at every turn. If it's

Church, then he will try to have your boss ask you every week if you can work on Sunday and make you feel condemned if you don't work. So, he wants you to think that you are a bad Christian if you tell your boss no because you are supposed to honor and obey those in authority according to the Bible. But if you do work, then you suffer because you don't get to go to Church. He will try to make it impossible for you to do the right thing. But if you fight back and make a stand against the enemy, then you will be blessed by God, and He will protect you.

You are to obey the Word of God before any man or authority. Missing out on Church is such a victory for the enemy if you fall into that trap. I am sure the demons get rewarded for every Christian they can keep out of Church every Sunday. I can't help but mention "The Screwtape Letters" by C.S. Lewis. I just read some of that book the other day. It exposes how Satan's Kingdom is very strategic and deliberate about how they manipulate Christians. It is a fictional account of how demons talk to humans and get humans to sin or avoid the things of God. It is very descriptive and informative about how demons talk to us and suggest something in our thoughts.

The Devil deceives us by making us think that the thoughts we have about a subject are our own. This can condemn us if it is an evil thought. We have to be very careful to determine which voice we are listening to at any specific time. When you fast, it is a lot easier to discern what voice is speaking to you. Just to remind you, there is the Voice of God, your voice, and the enemy's voice. The enemy can use your voice and other people's voice. God can do the same thing. So, if you want to try to simplify it, then Hollywood has done an ok job. There is a demon on one shoulder and God on the other. Our voice is deceiving as well. We must take and submit all of our thoughts to the Lord, 2 Corinthians 10:5, "_We demolish arguments and every pretension that sets itself up against the knowledge of God, and we take captive every thought to make it obedient to Christ._" We have to not fall into the trap of fearful agreement and just let the enemy take over our thoughts. We have to fight Him with the Word of God. He wants to bully you, but you can't let him do that anymore. The Bible says that we must fight the good fight of faith!

The enemy's job is to deceive you and make you diluted. If you are a strong Church member that is involved in the Church and knocking on doors and leading people to the Lord, then you are a problem for the Devil. If you are a nursery worker that is a volunteer at the Church, then you are also a huge problem to the Devil. You are allowing people to serve God uninterrupted and then the kids get to learn about Jesus. So, you are a big target. Don't get discouraged when you get attacked. Go to God and get the Fruits of the Spirit to overcome the enemy. Galatians 5:22-25 lists the Fruits of the Spirit, which come from spending time with God,

> *"But the fruit of the Spirit is love, joy, peace, longsuffering, kindness goodness, faithfulness, gentleness, self-control. Against such, there is no law. And those who are Christ's have crucified the flesh with its passions and desires. If we live in the Spirit, let us also walk in the Spirit."*

The Devil loves to get people to think that they are smarter than God. It sounds crazy, but here is a way that the enemy does it. When we read Scripture about fornication the Devil tries to pervert It. A synonym of pervert is to lead astray. God says it is wrong to have sex outside of marriage. So, we look at sex and think God is withholding something good from us just like Eve thought in the garden. The Devil starts to say sex is ok. He says you can do other things besides sex. Then it escalates to sex. Before you know it, you have sex every day or have moved in with the person. This is a sin.

Rebellion against the Word of God is sin. The Bible says that sin has consequences. If you are a Christian, then you are saved, but you will face the consequences of this World from the enemy or from God. God chastises those whom He loves. God will correct us, and sometimes it hurts very much. He will use many different ways to correct us, and it could be the Police. We have to respect the Word of God. If we do, then we won't have to worry about all of the consequences our actions have from disobedience. But we think that we are smarter than God sometimes, and we have to push these boundaries. It is incredibly stupid to believe that we are more intelligent than God. But rest assured I have done this repeatedly in the past. It is best to just surrender to God than be swallowed up by a giant fish that is sent by God to retrieve you like the Prophet Jonah. Albert Einstein said, "The definition of insanity is doing the same thing over and over again and expecting different results." Lord, help us to stop being so prideful in our rebellion and just listen to You!

The enemy in some area of our lives has deceived us all. It doesn't matter if it is a Doctrine, sin habits, or anything else. We have been lied to, and we have believed the lie, or just refused to fight and just accept it. Now we have what we call "My truth." This is a terrible deception of the enemy. We call it "My truth" so that it cannot be refuted or proven wrong. This allows the deception to grow and spiral out of control. We refuse sound logic and reason. We reject the Wisdom of the Scriptures and with pride, hold onto a lie too tight. This is poison and will kill our progression of faith and obedience toward God. We have to repent and give up "Our truth" and submit it to the Word of God. We have to repent. Repent means to bring a sinful habit to God confess it and leave it with God. Then turn and walk away from the sin and stop doing it again. Prayer, in one sense, is bringing our garbage to God and confessing it and leaving it with Him, and He forgives us and disposes of it.

We need prayer, so the Devil won't deceive us. As you read in this book, you will see many areas that the Devil has deceived you and how he has achieved it. You will see that when this happens, we open the door to Satan, and he has a legal right to be in our lives because of unconfessed sin. We must go to God and ask Him to show us all the ways we have been deceived and daily repent from these things. We must change our minds to daily be conformed to the Mind of Christ. The Bible says we must daily transform our minds by reading the Word of God.

Let's pray and ask God's Help. "Father, please forgive me for my sinful choices. Please forgive me for allowing the enemy to have control of my thoughts and actions. Forgive me of my rebellion. I need Your help, and I ask that You to Break the Contract of Deception off of my life the enemy has placed on me. Help me to understand Your Word and to follow You with all of my heart. I renounce the lies of the enemy toward the Word of God and toward You God. Satan I renounce you as my master. I will no longer follow you. Please Lord help me to identify the voices that are talking to me daily. Help me to fight against the enemy's voice and follow Your Voice. In Jesus Name, I pray Amen." Let's keep learning how to get closer to God by defeating Satan in the next chapter!

CHAPTER 4

The Contract of Pride

"For though we walk in the flesh, we do not war according to the flesh. For the weapons of our warfare are not carnal but mighty in God for pulling down strongholds, casting down arguments and every high thing that exalts itself against the knowledge of God, bringing every thought into captivity to the obedience of Christ." 2 Corinthians 10:3-5

P ride is an ugly sin. Satan is the King of Pride. It says in the Bible, several times that he wants to be worshiped and that he wants to be like God. Isaiah 14:13-15 says,

"For you have said in your heart: 'I will ascend into heaven, I will exalt my throne above the stars of God; I will also sit on the mount of the congregation On the farthest sides of the north; I will ascend above the heights of the clouds, I will be like the Most High.' Yet you shall be brought down to Sheol, To the lowest depths of the pit."

Satan declared that he would be in a position of power. He decided in his heart and spoke with his mouth. However, the end of his prideful attempts will bring him to the lowest depths of the pit. He is full of pride, and the enemy wants us to fall into the same trap that he has fallen into. The only way to get rid of pride is to confess and repent. The Devil will not turn from his pride, so he will meet his end in the pit just as the Bible declares. The Biblical definition of pride means to believe that you are smarter than God and believe that you don't have to obey Him. Having pride in how clean your house is, on the other hand, can be

35

normal. But your motives will reveal the evil pride that elevates you above others or God. We are to be humble while serving God and one another. We are not to be idolized like Satan wants.

The Bible says in Proverbs 9:10, "*The fear of the Lord is the beginning of wisdom.*" Satan does not fear the Lord because he defied Him and has launched a full-on attack against Him in every way. Satan is the perfect example of pride and its consequences. God will allow Satan and us to walk in pride. However, there is a pit awaiting anyone who walks in pride. We have all heard that pride comes before a fall. The Scripture is Proverbs 16:18, "*Pride goes before destruction and a haughty spirit before a fall.*" Pride doesn't just happen. Satan tempts us to be prideful like him. Temptations come from the enemy and our flesh. Our flesh has desires and wants us to fulfill them, no matter what.

The flesh does not care if your sanctification (Obedience to God) is compromised or stopped. It wants what it wants, right now! The way the flesh behaves reminds me of the kid, Violet, from the movie "Willy Wonka and the Chocolate Factory." She wanted the candy that was a complete meal before it was ready for the market. It was not safe, and Wonka warned her, but she ate it regardless. She had severe consequences and blew up bigger than her ego. She had to be escorted to the juicing room to be juiced down to regular size by the Oompa Loompas. The Bible warns us that pride leads to destruction. However, do we care? Not if we are acting in pride!

Pride is a deception that we put on like blinders that horses wear. When the enemy deceives us, we agree to the Contract of Pride. The Contract of Pride has many unfortunate consequences that we have already seen. We allow pride to shackle us like a binding contract. Contracts can be fun if you inherit money, and you agree to a contract to enable you to have the money awarded to you yearly for the rest of your life. You are continually getting a blessing for the rest of your life. However, when the contract has nothing but torment day after day, the contract will make you miserable. You are chained to the contract even though you didn't understand all of the ramifications of what pride does to you.

Pride deceives you into being limited to your knowledge and the limited knowledge the enemy shares with you. Pride will lead to destruction, but it also brings with it a whole host of nasty attitudes. The haughty spirit, as the Bible describes, is just hostile. When you see someone being arrogant or prideful, it is a bad look. You just hope that they are right because if not, they are headed for destruction. Overconfident is a synonym of haughty. Therefore, when you are overconfident and fail at something, it is time to come back to the drawing board and see what went wrong. Sadly, with pride, you do not have this luxury if you continue in it. You only readjust a few things and continue in your arrogance. No one can tell you that you are going the wrong way because you have decided that pride will be your GPS. Pride will never ask you to reconsider your actions. Accepting pride from the enemy is a trap that can last forever.

You have to come to the point that you realize that you are not smarter than God. The Devil has not reached this place. He just keeps trying to outsmart God and thinks this will work. God has had infinite eternities to put a lot of thought into His Word. He is not going to be proven wrong. We have all learned that God is right. When we heard the Gospel of Jesus and we accepted the Word of God, we found out that Jesus was the Son of God. We felt Him come into our hearts and we felt our sin being lifted off of us. We knew that God and His Word were not to be trifled with. However, as we walk in the Christian Faith, we have an enemy that slowly wants to turn us away from God. He is very effective, and God wants us to repent before it is too late. Pride will destroy you because it will not let you see the end result of your actions. Only Wisdom from the Lord will protect you from the plan of the enemy. It's hard to repent when walking in pride because you are blind. The Bible says we become stiff necked rebellious people whose end is destruction.

It does not matter in what way you rebel against God it is evil. What is worse a Witch or a Scientist that does not believe in God? Both will go to hell if they do not repent for their sins. The Witch is possibly looking for power and wants to play around with spells. The Scientist wants to play around with formulas and hypothesize on how to figure out the secrets of the Universe. The Big Bang Theory is promoted by Scientists. This theory says that something exploded and all of creation was formed by the explosion of matter. But more importantly is who created the thing that exploded? Scientists spend their whole lives trying to disprove God is the Creator. They hang on to theories and their desperate hypothesis. They allow pride to take over and it will cause them to be an enemy of God.

Pride brings rebellion. You choose a side when you choose pride. I am not saying that you lose your salvation, but you are walking with the enemy closer than the Lord. Pride takes you away from the things of God and God himself. God will never leave us or forsake us, but sin takes us away from a close relationship with God. We get lost in our sin and backslide away from God.

These are all cute terms that describe rebellion. This is not a children's book with pop-ups, so I think you are old enough to hear the truth. We are responsible for our actions. I am accountable for my actions. I know that what I do either good or bad will reap a harvest one way or another. The Bible says that what a man sows he will reap. It is only by God's Grace that we do not die every time we choose to rebel against God.

Pride puts you on the throne and takes God off the throne. Pride is rebellion toward God, and rebellion is described as witchcraft in 1 Samuel 15:23, "*For rebellion is as the sin of witchcraft, And stubbornness is as iniquity and idolatry because you have rejected the word of the Lord.*" Sin is rebellion toward God. God describes rebellion as witchcraft. It's eye-opening for the Lord to make this comparison because we are blinded to this fact when we are in rebellion. Therefore, rebellion is practicing evil. God is Holy, and He wants us to practice righteousness. Practicing righteousness is obeying the Lord. Practicing witchcraft is disobeying the Lord. Don't shoot the messenger! If you are in sin in any area of your life, you know that you are holding onto darkness. This darkness will manifest itself in sin and rebellion. Witchcraft and sin are not a joke. These activities bring demons, strongholds, oppression, and attacks from the enemy. Pride will blind you to all evil that you are practicing or obeying.

Strongholds are demonic mindsets that are controlling an area of your life with your permission. When you accept a demonic thought or theology, then the demon now has a nest (Demonic Stronghold) forming in your mind. When agreed with, these thoughts will reprogram your mind, transforming it into an evil machine programmed to do the Devil's will. When you choose to sin in a specific area of your life, you allow the enemy to continue to build the nest. Eventually, you have eggs that have hatched birds, and more nests. Your mind will be so clouded by demonic activity that you will be confused and blinded to God's Word. Have you ever read a part of the Bible and thought, wow, no one could obey God in that way or it is too hard to do? This is another trap of the enemy that is telling you that you do not have to submit to that part of the Bible because it is impossible. The enemy only allows you to submit to the parts of the Bible that are easy or meaningless to you, so you aren't a threat to him. We must rebuke every thought that the enemy tells us no matter what.

Have you ever been lost using GPS, it suggests a way to go, and you go in a different direction because you think it is a better route? Maybe I am the only person that has done that. We are prone to being prideful even as Christians.

Pride is a lifelong struggle. We have a choice every day to be prideful or humble. The only way we can get closer to God is to choose to be humble and submit to His Word no matter what we think. I need to apologize to your ego. I am going to propose some hard truths for you to swallow, but you will be ok. Spoiler alert, we have to realize that our perception is not always correct. Reread that sentence until you understand it. Your way is not always right! Sometimes other people have the proper perspective. God always has the right perspective. He has given it to us in the form of the Bible. If we want to see if we are deceived or prideful, then all we have to do is open up God's Word and start reading. If our thoughts or actions do not match exactly with what the Word of God says, then we need to repent! It is simple. God is right, and your theories or opinions are wrong! Isaiah 55:8-9 says,

"For My thoughts are not your thoughts, Nor are your ways My ways, says the Lord. For as the heavens are higher than the earth, So are My ways higher than your ways, And My thoughts than your thoughts."

The Bible is true, no matter what you think or how you feel about it. So why am I hammering this into your head? That is a good question, and the answer is because of pride. Prideful people do not listen. Therefore, it is best to repeat things from 10 different perspectives so they will eventually see it. Remember that when you think the World is falling apart from your perspective. Go and talk to 10 people, and you will know that you had a one-sided view. Most of the time, you hear people say, "It could always be worse!" This is true. I am trying to free your mind. In Jesus Name, open your eyes! If you are in pride, then you are a crash-test dummy. You are heading for a brick wall, and you will crash. Pride is noticeable a mile away to everyone but you, of course. Pride is not satisfying; it is exhausting. You don't' always have to be right! Sin destroys our life, and pride allows the enemy to come into our lives without resistance, Proverbs 25:28 says, "*Whoever has no rule over his own spirit is like a city broken down, without walls.*" If your city has no protection, anyone can pass over your walls, do whatever they want to your city, and take it over with no resistance. You must get rid of the thing that destroyed the walls of your city or temple.

God is giving you a way out of this disaster. Do not silence the GPS of God. He is trying to show you the way out if you would only follow the path. You can't compromise your way around God. You cannot compromise your way through the Bible. You are deceiving yourself if you continue to think that you are smarter than God. Rebellion is sin, and it is sinful not to obey the Word of God. Are you deceived? How can you tell? According to James 1:22, there is a surefire way to tell, "*But be doers of the word, and not hearers only, deceiving yourselves.*" Here are some ways to do a test to see if you are operating in pride and rebellion. Are you ready? Ok. Do you believe that the Word of God is Absolute Truth, but do not obey it thoroughly in every area of your life? Do you think that you are in sin right now in any area of your life? Do you avoid reading the Word of God? Do you avoid Christian activities? Do you avoid Church? Do you hate hearing about God sometimes? Do you ever avoid praying to Jesus? Do you feel like you could be closer to God than you are right now?

If you answered yes to any of those questions, then you are prideful and rebellious in your life in some way. Now we have to remember that disobeying God is a sin. Sin is comparable to witchcraft, according to God. The Word of God is our guide to obeying God. God has mercy waiting for you when you admit your pride and repent. God loves you and does not want you to crash your life. He also wants to have a close intimate relationship with Him, but sin gets in the way. Dwight L. Moody said, "The Bible will keep you from sin, or sin will keep you from the Bible." When we sin, it pulls us away from God and makes us even forget about God temporarily and condemns us. When we get close to God, then we forget about sin and enjoy God and being free.

When you hear people saying, "I am spiritual, not religious," it is their way of saying that they do not follow any rules. They have no Absolute Truth and are in rebellion. Choose this day who you will serve. Humility is the only way out of sin. We must realize that our sin is displeasing to God, and I know that you want to please Him. Jesus says, "My burden is easy, and my yoke is light." He wants you to serve Him. It is not stress-free or problem-free because Jesus said that in this World, we will have trouble. However, He says to rejoice because He has overcome the World. Sin can give you a calloused heart, but you have to realize that pride is evil, and the Devil wants to kill you. You must clear your conscience before God (1 Peter 3:16). If you hear the Voice of the Lord and repent, He will forgive you and restore your life. He has good plans for you, but He cannot bless you the way He wants to if you are disobeying Him. Jump into His Lap and let Him love on you.

Let's pray and break the Contract of Pride. I want you to make a list of all of the ways that you have been prideful toward the Lord. As a life practice you should ask other people you know what you are being prideful about in your life. You can be humble and learn from them. They may be right. If not it is a humbling experience to consider another person's perspective. Try to think of all of the things that you have done in the past that were prideful. He will show you. However, you need to be thorough so you can break the Contract of Pride. Once you have the list, then we will pray over it. Don't worry about how long it is. You may be writing for an hour or two. Just make sure that you listen to the Lord. It could just be half a page.

Write out how you were prideful and in what ways or activities you have been prideful. Especially write down how you have been prideful to people and God. I have made an outline at the end of the book for you to use right now. Go complete it and get ready to pray. The Lord will set you free, and the Contract of Pride will be broken if you obey the Lord in this way. James 4:6 says, "*But he gives us more grace.*" The Scriptures say God opposes the proud but gives grace to the humble. God will bless your obedience. James 4:10 says, "*Humble yourselves before the Lord, and He will lift you up.*"

Let's pray over the list you have. Pray this and repeat it out loud. "Heavenly Father, I come to you in humility. I see that I have been prideful in my life. I have rebelled against You, and I am sorry. I confess my sinful actions to You. I have listed out many evil things I have done in pride. Help me now in breaking the sin of pride in my life. Lord, please forgive me of my sins. I renounce all of the sins of pride in my life. I break the Contract of Pride over my life that I signed with the enemy in Jesus Name. Satan leave my life right now. You have no right to be in my life. I repent from pride and sin and ask You, Lord, to fill me with your Spirit and help me to serve You in Jesus Name. Amen." Let us continue to the next chapter to learn about the Contract of Wrath. The Lord is breaking the chains and setting us free!

CHAPTER 5

The Contract of Wrath

"And be kind to one another, tenderhearted, forgiving one another, even as God in Christ forgave you." Ephesians 4:32

Praise the Lord! It is a great day to be free in Jesus. God is amazing, and the Joy of the Lord is your strength! I just want to brag on Jesus because He sets the captives free. Once you leave jail and cross the threshold of the Jailhouse doors, you are free. You are no longer tortured with the burden of being told what to do 24/7. Jail is only a temporary situation. You can make a phone call and be bonded out. It is a temporary place if you have the money to be bailed out. Now in some cases, you are denied bail, and you have to wait on the judge to decide on your fate. In this case, you can be set free or found guilty and sent to prison. Now prison is the next step to jail. Prison is where you get transferred from jail to a long-term sentence of punishment. There is no hope for bail in prison. You can get an early release if you have good behavior or get parole. Otherwise, you have to complete your entire sentence no matter what! When we don't forgive others, we are trapped in jail, and if we continue in this sin, we will be put in the prison of unforgiveness by the enemy.

The Bible tells us that out of the abundance of the heart, the mouth speaks. We try, but we cannot control our mouths. What the heart wants the heart speaks about out loud. If you listen to a person, you can hear about their problems or intentions. The Bible says that we are to be quick to hear James 1:19-20 says, "*So then, my beloved brethren, let every man be swift to hear, slow to speak, slow to wrath; for the wrath of man does not produce the righteousness of God.*" We are to be quick to hear! Cool. I heard exactly what that person called me and now

I'm going to beat him up! Thanks, Pastor! NO! This is not what this text is saying! We are to be quick to hear; if you have the Spirit of God and your discernment is sharp, then you can hear who is speaking to you through that person. Remember, I told you the voices that speak to you are God, yourself, and the enemy. Well, the Lord uses us, and so does the Devil. We wrestle not against flesh and blood, but against demons, the Bible tells us. Therefore, when we hear the enemy's voice speaking to us through someone, we have a choice to make. Do we turn the other cheek and respond in love and humility? There is power in a softly spoken word Proverbs 15:1 says, "<u>A gentle answer turns away wrath, but a harsh word stirs up anger. The tongue of the wise commends knowledge, but the mouth of the fool spouts folly.</u>"

A gentle spirit is the way to go when dealing with a fool. The mouth of the fool spouts anything he thinks in his head. There is no mouth filter for a fool. His heart is so corrupted that he has no filter because he has allowed the enemy to pollute it. Proverbs 18:6, "<u>A fool's lips walk into a fight, and his mouth invites a beating.</u>" A filter for your mouth could save your life. A harsh word stirs up wrath, but are you prepared for the enemy's wrath coming through someone else? You say "YES, BRING IT ON", and then you get shot and die in your arrogance. What then? Everyone will see what a fool you were for running your mouth. Your close friends on social media and strangers will have a field day laughing at you to scorn about how you couldn't control your mouth. Now it is time to repent before you leave the earth too soon. There is always someone bigger than you are, and His Name is Jesus. You will be judged for every word that comes out of your mouth! James says, the no one can tame the tongue, and it is set on fire from hell. The battle starts in your mind with your thoughts. Watch your mouth by watching your thoughts. Submit all thoughts to God. Just because you can say something doesn't mean that you should!

Let's start talking about wrath in the Word of God as it progresses from its beginning stages. Now wrath begins with a person holding unforgiveness. The Bible has a solution to this problem in Matthew 18:21-22,

"Then Peter came to Him and said, "Lord, how often shall my brother sin against me, and I forgive him? Up to seven times?" Jesus said to him, "I do not say to you, up to seven times, but up to seventy times seven."

Peter mentions forgiving a person seven times if they have committed sin against him. However, Jesus takes that to the moon. Peter, I'm sure dropped his jaw! The reason I say that is the Jewish custom at the time was that you should forgive your brother three times a day. Therefore, Peter doubled it and added 1 for good measure. He thought this would be satisfactory because Jesus had higher standards. Jesus told him no way! Seventy times seven is 490 times. I did the math so you can realize that you have no excuse for holding unforgiveness toward someone. Four hundred ninety times can be exceeded if you are offended easily or if the other person is a terrible person, but this was not a lifetime sum. This was to be applied per day.

Now it is our responsibility to forgive. I suggest doing it immediately, but that takes practice and prayer. We are human, so we get offended, and it hurts. When we get injured and cut our finger, it takes time to heal naturally. However, if not properly attended to, it will get infected. The infection could result in amputation or death. Forgiveness is not the easiest thing to do. My old Bible College Professor told us, "Forgiveness is a miracle." I genuinely believe that with all of my heart. We have to let the Love of God flow through us so we can forgive that person. Forgiveness is not just a quick action; I wish that were the case. Forgiveness is a full-time job. I say this because when we decide to forgive a person, then the Devil challenges us to make sure we are serious about our decision. He burdens us with always thinking about the offense. We can't get into worship or through the day without images or voices of what the person did or said to us out of our minds. The images continue to burrow until they take root at the very core and take us over. We must allow God to stop the root from growing through repentance.

The Devil will cause us to get lost in our offense. When someone offends us, we immediately feel the injury. Our pride is assaulted. We start to think, "Wow, I can't believe they just did that!" If you are like me, then I will call someone to tell them what has happened. This is my way of venting, but it usually turns into a gossip fest that just makes me angrier. Oh, and I have to mention that when I choose to do this, it spreads sin to other people. The reason I say that is that when I call my friend to tell them what happened, they are now tempted to get offended as well. Typically, my friend is having a good day, and for him, the birds are singing, and the sun is shining, and he is having a Mary Poppins experience just lost in happiness. Then I call with a dark cloud of lightning and thunder with high winds and a hailstorm. I unload on him, and then usually, his mood changes from happy to giving me the advice to go and beat someone up. He will tell me that he is ready to go and help right now. I wonder what kind of issues he has to where he is prepared to "Hulk Out" at any moment. I will give him a copy of this book so he will be fine. It's ok to laugh; we all know someone like this! Keep praying for them.

Therefore, when we choose to get offended, it affects other people. I don't know how often I have been talking to someone about how I was treated in a particular situation, and they get madder than I am. I have been asked by people to give them the address to the person that has treated me wrong. These people are serious, and I wonder if they don't have a shovel in their trunk at all times to bury a body if needed. The Bible says that we should be instant in season and out of season to be ready to preach the Gospel. However, these types of people are prepared to murder and cover it up like it's just another day of the week. I'm sure that you have run across someone like this, or maybe it is you. This is the result of allowing past offenses to turn into wrath. Once your anger has reached wrath and remains untreated, anything can set you off to DEFCON 1.

To prevent a World War, it is best to get a hold of this thing before it takes off. If you are on the ledge right now, then don't look down! Look up and allow God to heal you. There is a commercial that I think is hilarious. In the commercial, a guy is sitting in his living room, all alone comfortably watching cable and relaxing, and then the cable gets interrupted. He has to call the cable guy and he realizes that it is going to take forever for him to show up. Then the guy starts peering out the window into the neighborhood because he is bored. He sees a car next door, and two ruggedly suspicious shady guys are loading a body shaped figure wrapped in a roll of carpet into a trunk. They look up to see him staring at them, and he quickly ducks his head and pulls the drapes. He goes to the extreme because of fear and panic, and he packs a bag, and it switches to a cut scene of a boat on fire in the middle of the ocean and him swimming away as he fakes his death so they would think he is dead. Therefore, I explained that to say that you should make sure you are doing the right thing at all times because the enemy is ready to punish you if you are idle. The guy was just looking out a window for no reason. He could have picked up his Bible and spent time with God. However, the Devil had another plan for him.

So, tying this all together is the fact that you will be punished if you do what the enemy wants you to do. You will wind up in jail or running for your life because you stuck your nose in something that should have been left alone, and it did not turn out the way that you thought it would. It's as if you get cut off by someone on the road, and you follow that person and honk until they pull over. You are so mad that you have decided you will give this person a tongue-lashing and beat them up. You pull up, four doors open up, and four guys get out with Karate Gis on and start to chase after you until they all four practice their martial arts skills on you like a dummy at their dojo. There are consequences to grabbing the Devil's hand at the beginning stage of the offense and allowing him to take you and drop you off at wrath. You lose every time. You might think that you are winning the game at some point, but you are the one being played.

Anger is the first step in this process. The Bible says to take action quickly when you are offended. Ephesians 4:26-27 says, "*Be angry, and do not sin, do not let the sun go down on your wrath, nor give place to the devil.*" Therefore, we see here the Bible says that anger is ok, but what we do with it can lead to sin. Don't let the sun go down means forgive right away. If it's 5 pm, then we only have a few hours until the sun goes down. We are not to enjoy being mad until the sun goes down and then forgive. Forgive right away because the enemy is the one wanting you to be offended. We are allowed to be angry at sin or the enemy but not with another person. Ephesians 6:12 says, "*For we do not wrestle against flesh and blood, but against principalities, against powers, against the rulers of the darkness of this age, against spiritual hosts of wickedness in the heavenly places.*"

The enemy is the one that uses a person or situation to get us offended. The other person is just a pawn in the whole process. With this perspective, you can see that the Devil is continually using people and situations to try to get us offended. Now, if the other person is godly, then they will realize what is happening as well and will not allow the Devil to get his way. However, Christians still let the Devil do what he wants sometimes, and then everyone has to go back and apologize to each other, which he hates. However, our goal is to live a life free of offense as the Word of God says in Romans 12:18, "*If it is possible, as much as depends on you, live peaceably with all men.*" It is apparent in the Bible that it is up to us to take action and to control our anger. It is up to us to decide to forgive, and it is our responsibility to forgive no matter what. It is a sin if we do not forgive.

If we foolishly decide to move past anger, then we are signing a Contract of Wrath with the Devil. We are letting him into the front seat of the car and telling us where to go next turn by turn. This can eventually lead to demonic possession, so this Contract is severe. Ephesians 4:31 says we should forgive people even as Christ forgave us, *"Let all bitterness, wrath, anger, clamor, and evil speaking be put away from you, with all malice. And be kind to one another, tenderhearted, forgiving one another, even as God in Christ forgave you."* We are warned to get rid of all bitterness, wrath, anger, and evil speaking. We are to be tenderhearted, but when we choose to allow the anger and bitterness to take root, then we harden our hearts to the Voice of the Lord. We are to forgive others because Christ forgave us of all of our sins. Therefore, we have warnings and encouragements. Let's look at the progression of this sin and its consequences in the Contract.

Bitterness is the next phase of this nightmare of offense. When we get angry and let the sun go down on that anger, then it turns to bitterness. The enemy gets you to think about this offense every day. Anger opens a door for the enemy to have a place in our soul and mind. We have hired the enemy to torment us at this point. We have added to the contract his legal right to be in our life. It seems like there is nothing you can do about it at this point because pride has blinded you to taking the offense and becoming angry to the point of bitterness so that you will not let it go. It reminds me of a dog with a bone. The dog will not let go of it no matter how hard you try. The Devil slowly eats at you like cancer by replaying the offense. I know the Devil has played an offense in my mind like a movie. I saw it, and then at the point of the offense, it paused. I could see what that person did to me from a 360 degree angle like a football replay. It would make me even more hurt and angry; especially when the person did not care that they even hurt me.

This process just continues, and we feel justified with what we think is righteous anger because they did something sinful to us. The Devil gets us to really allow the hurt and bitterness to take root by showing us that we are a victim. How dare they do this to me! Our feelings and emotions get the best of us. I have always said, "Show me a person who is controlled by their emotions and I will show you a prisoner." The Devil uses our emotions to get us to act out in the flesh and punish people, "A person controlled by their emotions is a puppet for the enemy to use." The Devil gets us to become self-righteous, and then we get full of pride. When we retell the story or think about it, we hold back the parts of how we may have been at fault or what we did to escalate the situation. The Devil also makes us think that they are also mad at us because we have chosen to be angry at them. Then we get offended because we believe they are offended at us. He manipulates our perception in so many ways it's deceptive and confusing.

I have tried to tell someone who was offended at me that they wronged me in the same way in the past so they would realize I had forgiven them already, and they were just as guilty as I was. However, they turned it all around on me to make me look like the bad guy for bringing it up and saying that I had not let it go either. Wow! With this type of sin, people love to be a victim and blame you for being in the same sin as them! Sitting in the corner, licking their own wounds to the point of obsession. Then, the Devil comes along to be there for them and to be their best friend who listens to their sorrows. All of this evil is followed by pride, arrogance, and self-righteousness. The Lord declares in Romans 12:19, "*Never take your own revenge, beloved, but leave room for the wrath of God, for it is written, 'VENGEANCE IS MINE, I WILL REPAY,' says the Lord.*" We are warned again not to take revenge because it is an unbalanced unauthorized arena that is above our pay grade.

We are not to venture into the area of vengeance because it is for a Holy God to decide what type of punishment each offense requires. We cannot steal God's Scepter and hop on the Throne. We cannot play God thinking in our wrath, we know what is best for a just reward for the person who offended us! Most of the time, the answer would be what the Red Queen would say in the movie "Alice in Wonderland," "Off with his head!" In the film, the Red Queen simply caught someone eating something of hers, and she gave the order! Wow! We are to leave the room or back up and evacuate the area to make room for God's Wrath. God will not let someone get away with injustices forever. He will deal with them in this life, after they die or both! We are told to put down the fruit from the part of the garden that we have plucked and run from it. It will bring disaster to our lives because we now allow God to punish us for taking what is His. The warning sign reads, KEEP OUT! THE WRATH OF GOD IS STORED UP FOR ANYONE WHO CROSSES INTO THE AREA OF VENGEANCE!

We now move on from bitterness to unforgiveness. This is where we choose not to obey God and firmly hold what we try to justify as a grudge. This word grudge is a playground term. However, what we are doing is evil and witchcraft. Sure, we are justified in being angry. Instead of taking our anger to God and releasing it, we are opening a door for the enemy to pour wrath into our soul. This makes us turn dark as pitch in our souls. Ephesians 4:29 says,

"Let no corrupt word proceed out of your mouth, but what is good for necessary edification, that it may impart grace to the hearers. And do not grieve the Holy Spirit of God, by whom you were sealed for the day of redemption."

We can see here in this same passage that we have been studying that the Lord is warning us not to grieve the Holy Spirit. When we choose to harbor unforgiveness, then we are pushing God out of our minds and hearts. We are silencing the Voice of God. Nevertheless, the enemy tries to make us think that we are still close to God by deception. Therefore, here is another opportunity for us to humble ourselves and submit to the Word of God. The Bible says in 1 John 4:20-21,

"If someone says, "I love God," and hates his brother, he is a liar; for he who does not love his brother whom he has seen, how can he love God whom he has not seen? And this commandment we have from Him: that he who loves God must love his brother also."

So now, the Word of God says that since we were hurt and angered by the offense, we are currently not close to God anymore. No! When you choose to stay angry and not forgive, then you push God out and invite the Devil inside. Then you are in disobedience and sin. Then you must choose to repent, or you will be filled with wrath. The Bible says that if you say you love God, then you are a liar because you have hate in your heart for someone.

When you make the firm decision not to forgive the person, then this turns to hate, and the demonic activity really starts to heat up. Hating someone leads to violent speech and actions. There are many different ways to act out this hatred toward someone. We can be verbally aggressive, physically aggressive, or passively aggressive. Now many Scriptures speak about how we should forgive, but in this stage, it is harder to come back because we have hardened our hearts toward the Voice of God, which is telling us to forgive and love the person. Jesus even said that we should love instead of hate in Matthew 5:43-44,

"You have heard that it was said, 'You shall love your neighbor and hate your enemy.' But I say to you, love your enemies, bless those who curse you, do good

to those who hate you, and pray for those who spitefully use you and persecute you,"

We have to pray for our enemies. I knew that when I fell deep in this trap in my 20's, I felt the cloud of darkness try to come into my soul, and I didn't like it. I enjoyed playing the victim and having people feel sorry for me, but when the demons tried to come in to stay, I rejected them.

I had to pray for my enemy because I knew I didn't want to go forward with wrath. I had reached a crossroads and turned to the Lord. I knew what I had to do, and it was hard. I had put so much effort into hating them that I was mad that I had to repent. It had become part of my identity and personality. I had to repent from the power I felt when I was walking with these spirits. It created a power inside of me that would be a fiery furnace of anger. I would intimidate people, and they would be scared of me because of the demons that I was carrying around with me. People knew there was something different with me, and I didn't even go all the way to the point of possession.

When you get to the point of wrath, there is a certain power that can be intoxicating. You can feel empowered by darkness, and it tries to take over your very person by acting out its agenda through you toward anybody that comes in your path. The enemy now has a complete foothold and is waiting for any opportunity to use you for its will like a puppet master. At this stage, you can be set off by anything, and it causes you to start gathering offenses, whether it is your offenses that happen to you or something that happened to someone else. You are just gathering more hate and anger on top of your unforgiveness. This leads to wrath. When the contract has nothing but torment day after day, the contract will make you miserable. You are chained to the contract even if you don't understand all of the ramifications of what wrath does to you.

There may be times of blackouts and fights that you could experience. The Devil has your heart, and so he has your speech as well. It is nothing for someone to spout off the evilest things ever uttered and not think twice about it. In this state, the person is full of evil and is not listening or following God in a close relationship. They can still be nice but only for selfish reasons. This leads to religious spirits that come in to tell you that you are still following God, and everything is fine. You can even be a functioning religious Christian just going through the motions. Still, all along, you are being tormented by what that person did to you and focusing on that hurt and being fueled by anger and hate continually. It is exhausting and tormenting. As Jesus says, you will be penniless when it is all over because you will pay the price for choosing not to forgive Matthew 5:23-26,

> *"Therefore, if you bring your gift to the altar, and there remember that your brother has something against you, leave your gift there before the altar and go your way. First, be reconciled to your brother, and then come and offer your gift. Agree with your adversary quickly, while you are on the way with him, lest your adversary delivers you to the judge, the judge hand you over to the officer and you be thrown into prison. Assuredly, I say to you, you will by no means get out of there till you have paid the last penny."*

Walking with Satan and obeying His Contract is torture on you and the other people you know, but there is hope in Jesus. Jesus says that being a Christian is not going to be a cakewalk, but His Yoke is easy, and the burden is light. This means following and obeying Jesus is not always easy, but it is freeing and brings Joy. However, the Devil's yoke is exhausting, and it is a continuous burden that ends up with demon possession or oppression. This will cause you to damage your relationships with your family and friends. You can lose your marriage and your freedom. You can get mad and offended at Pastors, Churches, Christians, and other people who have tried to help you. I have seen people even become angry at organizations indirectly. If you are a toxic person, no one wants to be around you because all you do is leak hatred and judgment out of your mouth, and you don't see any problem with it. You have chosen your side, and it is making people around you uncomfortable, but maybe they don't say anything because they do not know how to approach you or what to say. However, the Word of God says that you must repent. You have to make a choice to serve God and remove the Devil out of your life.

You have heard that, "If you don't have anything good to say, then you should not say anything at all" right? It came from the Bible in Ephesians 4:29,

> *"Let no corrupt word proceed out of your mouth, but what is good for necessary edification, that it may impart grace to the hearers. And do not grieve the Holy Spirit of God, by whom you were sealed for the day of redemption."*

We must also dispel the rumor that I will forgive, but I will never forget! 1 Corinthians 13:4-6 says,

> *"Love is patient; love is kind. It does not envy; it does not boast; it is not proud. It does not dishonor others; it is not self-seeking; it is not easily angered; it keeps no record of wrongs. Love does not delight in evil but rejoices with the truth. It always protects, always trusts, always hopes, always perseveres."*

Therefore, love keeps no record of wrong. We must choose to be like God and forget the evil that was committed.

Wrath turns into a perpetual murderous Spirit that is desperately willing to do anything to further fuel itself. We cannot continue in this sin and allow the enemy to use our mouth and soul. There are people I know that continually enable the enemy to use their mouths, which drives me mad because they are sinning, and the enemy has an open door to attack me because I choose to be there friend and hang out with them. It grieves the Holy Spirit from using them, and it grieves the Holy Spirit from blessing the relationships they have. They cut themselves off from God being able to use them. The Bible says to not associate with people who have fully committed to sin because you will learn their ways. Love them from a distance and pray for them that they will repent from the evil roots they have allowed to grow deep and robust. The Devil's Contract can be broken, but it will take the miracle of forgiveness.

The Lord showed me that a person who is offended is like an animal wounded on the side of the road. When you approach it you see that it is injured and trying to protect itself from further injury. You come along trying to help the animal but it growls at you and tries to bite you. The animal will not understand that you are trying to help it. It would rather bleed to death than allow you to get close to help it. You may have to try a different tactic to help it or call for help by using emergency services. We don't know exactly how they got injured. It could have been by a car running it over or other animals beating it up trying to kill it. It will bite you if you try to move it to safety or help it so be careful. The animal is ignorant to the fact that it is going to bleed out and die. It is just suffering in its pain and trying to avoid further injuries.

A person is just like this wounded animal. We don't know all of the circumstances that caused the injuries but we notice they are wounded. We notice they need help and are being defensive and are refusing help. They are just straight painful to be around. We can try to help them but if we get bit by them then we are not to shoot the person and put them out of their misery. The Devil loves it when Christians get mad at other Christians who are lost in wrath or bitterness. We have to allow the Lord to guide us in helping them and allow His Love to flow through us while ministering to them (1 Corinthians 13:4-7). We have to realize that the enemy will lash out at us because he has a stronghold in their lives and we are engaging in spiritual warfare when we try to recover the stolen ground the enemy has taken in their lives. We have to call on God to change their heart so we can help them. Until they acknowledge the past injuries or offenses and see that it is wrong then they can't be helped. We can sow seeds by using the Word of God and pray but that is it. Satan will lash out at us and try to bite us but we have to use the Wisdom and Spirit of God to fight back.

Once a person is this far along, they have been consumed by these demonic spirits, and their personality has been compromised. The demons have been active for too long, and people are afraid to repent because there is a void created when they remove Satan from their lives. I have been part of a demonic possession where there were three demons inside of a woman. I was asked by a Muslim man to cast the demons out of his wife because everyone is his Religion could not do it. He was a devout Muslim, and for him to ask me, this was out of desperation. However, I worked for him at the time, and he always heard me on the phone talking about casting out demons and the Power of Jesus Christ.

I showed up with a close friend, and we, after much warfare, cast out the spirits. We ministered until all demons had been cast out, and her eye color went from black to green. She was frightened because she didn't know who we were, yet we had been there for hours. Her husband hugged her, and they started talking. She asked how her kids were doing, and then we began to share the Gospel with her. She rejected the Gospel and said that she did not want the demons to leave because they were her friends. She immediately disappeared, and her eyes turned black again. She did not want Jesus and felt the demonic spirits offered a cherished friendship. How sad. She had been truly deceived.

When you decide to forgive, God's Power will protect you and remove Satan from your life. Therefore, you don't have to have someone to cast out demons from you. However, you need to make a list of all of the people that have wronged you. Once you make a list, next to their name, you should write what they did to you. In making this list, you should pray and ask the Lord who else you are holding unforgiveness toward, so the list is complete. It could be from your childhood until today. Make sure you include yourself and God. We get offended at things and people that don't even deserve it. We blame God because something in our life didn't go right, and we believe that God could have changed it or should have never allowed it to happen. The Devil is the god of this World. Bad things are going to happen. We have to proactively pray against the enemy to prevent this. An example is in the back of the book for you to use (Breaking the Devil's Contract of Wrath).

When you're writing your list, you want to make sure that you get every offense down. You must write down the person that you're offended at and everything that you can remember that causes you hurt and makes you angry or resentful about that person. I have made an outline at the end of the book for you to use. When I was a young Youth Pastor, I met with a person in the Church, who was a White Witch in the Church of Satan before he got saved. He had deliverance before at the Church through the elders, and I heard stories that they cast 20 demons out of them or something crazy.

One day he came up to me and asked me for help. He told me that he wanted to have demons cast out, and God said to him that I'm the person that needs to do it. I told him what the Holy Spirit was telling me, which is to make a list. He told me that he is mad at his sister. I told him he needs to write out a list of everything that she's ever done to him and what is currently offending him. Then he is to pray over the list and forgive her. He said that he was mad at her, and it had escalated to where he was planning on killing her. I told him to make that list, and I didn't need to cast any demons out of him. The Holy Spirit was telling me that if he would make a list, pray, and forgive the people he was offended at, then the demonic spirits would leave. Demons don't have a right to be in someone's life if you close the door they came in through.

I told him to pray about it and pray over the list, and he called me a few hours later and said that he had over three pages worth of stuff. I said, "Great now look at the Scriptures about forgiveness and study them." The Lord's Prayer talks about how we can be forgiven if we forgive those who sin against us. Right after the Lord's Prayer, Jesus says if you don't forgive those who sin against you; God will not forgive you of your sins. Therefore, God is making a bold statement about forgiveness. Forgiveness needs to be a priority in a Christian's life. I've heard it said that we need to have, "Thick skin and a soft heart." I told him to pray over the list because he had also been an emotional terrorist at some point in his life, and there are a lot of people he has offended.

He prayed over the list, went back, re-read everything out loud, and forgave his sister for the offenses. He was real about this. He poured his heart out into it. He was ready to deal with it. He called me after he got done and told me that he was healed. I forgot to mention, but whenever I met him at the restaurant, he came in hobbling on a cane, and he was pale white. I remember him not even being able to stand up because the pain was so bad. Right after he told me he was healed, I thought he got healed emotionally from the scars of unforgiveness only. When I saw him at Church, he didn't have the cane anymore; he didn't have any discoloration in his face and he looked normal. He was even doing jumping jacks in front of me. What a miracle! God is awesome. God did a miracle in his life because he repented. God had compassion on him and healed him completely. The Devil had such a stronghold in his life that it was crippling him and causing him bodily injury and pain. Once he forgave his sister, he got filled with God's Love, and it healed his body. The Kingdom of God came unto him. Whenever you have a visitation from God in the Bible Jesus says that the Kingdom of God has come unto you. Here is an example of a demonic contract of Wrath.

Example Contract of Wrath

I, <u>Karen</u> refuse to forgive Steve for the sins he has committed against me. I will not even consider forgiving Steve because the hurt and rejection is so painful that I am done with Steve. I give The Devil and his demons the right to occupy my mind and temple. I am choosing to accept unforgiveness, bitterness, hatred, and wrath as a mode of revenge for the offenses Steve has done to me. I allow The Devil to replay all offenses constantly. I allow The Devil to do this by showing me pictures of past offenses or scenarios that remind me of the offenses. I allow The Devil to replay audio clips of the offenses. I allow The Devil to do this anytime of the day or night even interrupting my sleep with dreams or not allowing me to sleep because of constant torture of the reminding me of the offenses.

I allow The Devil to help me plan revenge on him including the things that are important to him like his possessions, friends, and family. I allow the Devil to use my body parts to get revenge. I allow The Devil to have access to my mouth so I can spread this hatred and recruit anybody willing to help me get revenge. I allow The Devil access to my whole temple to make everyone around me bitter, depressed, or oppressed by the spirits that I have allowed to torture me. I allow my speech at anytime to be used by The Devil. I give The Devil the right to pour out wrath on anybody who has hurt, will hurt, or is hurting me now. I give up my peace and joy so I can constantly be bombarded with the oppression of hatred and wrath. I allow the Devil to use me in any way he sees fit to help me accomplish this goal. I give up my freedom and surrender to the plan of The Devil.

Signed,   Witnessed and Enforced By,

<u>Karen "The Prisoner"</u>   <u>The Devil "Satan"</u>

Let's Break the Contract of Wrath right now! Repeat this prayer out loud with all of your heart. "Heavenly Father, I come to You today in the precious Name of Jesus. Lord, I ask that You forgive me for all of my sins as I forgive those people who have sinned against me. Lord, I have been separated from You, and I am sorry. Right now, I want to lift this list up to You. I have been holding unforgiveness toward these people, and I ask, please forgive me. Your Word says that I'm supposed to forgive, and I was disobedient. I release these people from everything they have done to me. In Jesus Name, I renounce Satan and every root of offense, unforgiveness, rejection, and bitterness in my life. I break the Contract of Wrath in Jesus Name. I command every demonic spirit to leave right now and not come back. I close the door in Jesus Name, for any further demonic activity. Lord forgive me for my rebellion, and I pray that Your Love will purify my heart and heal me. Lord, help me to love and forgive people, and that I fall in love with You all over again. I accept Your Love in my life. Lord pour out Your Love to me. Allow me to use It to bless others. I allow Your Love to move though my temple and give It to everyone I have been offended at. I surrender to Love and will obey the Voice of Love. Thank you in Jesus Name, Amen."

Amen! If you made a list, asked the Lord to search your heart, and prayed to forgive all of those offenses, then you have been forgiven. You also have forgiven the offenses and emptied the Devil's belongings out of the room you gave him to stay. He is no longer dwelling in your house. You have filled up that room with the Love of God that covers a multitude of sins. When the Devil reminds you of an offense to get you reoffended, pray and ask God for the strength to forgive this person again. Put the sign out front that says, "No Vacancy, The Love of God is Here!"

We have to keep our guard up because the Devil loved living in your lovely furnished home with free room and board and will try to come back in through the same door again. He will plead, beg, and make anger, unforgiveness, and wrath look so appealing, but as James 4:7 says, "_Submit to God and resist the Devil, and he will flee from you!_" Fight the good fight of faith and send him packing every time he comes knocking on your door. Don't let him plant even one thought or seed in your head because it will eventually turn into a large tree that takes over your mind! You have already chopped down that tree and burned it, so don't grow another one like it!

CHAPTER 6

The Contract of Fear

"There is no fear in love, but perfect love casts out fear because fear involves torment. But he who fears has not been made perfect in love." 1 John 4:18

I have been Sonbathing for the last hour. It is incredible to soak up some rays of the Son. Yes, I said Son. I have been in the Presence of the Lord. How else am I able to talk to you about breaking the Contract of Fear! This is warfare, and it is serious, but I am a little drunk in the Spirit right now! Let me be clear; I do not drink alcohol. This is the New Wine that the Bible talks about in Ephesians 5:17-18, *"<u>Therefore, do not be unwise, but understand what the Will of the Lord is. And do not be drunk with wine, in which is dissipation, but be filled with the Spirit!</u>"* It feels good to be full of the Spirit. It leaves no room for the enemy with all of the torment and oppression that he wants to bring upon us. Jesus said His Yoke is easy, and His Burden is light. It is incredible to be free in Jesus. I am here to testify and give you hope of the one who sets the captives free, and His Name is JESUS! Now I am sure you don't read many books where people tell you that they have been worshiping the Lord right before they write to you. Relax and let the Lord minister to you through His Spirit.

I am writing to you with the Joy of the Lord today that fills my heart. Jesus has set me free from the things of this World that will choke the Word of God that is planted in my heart. I want to tell you about an evil spirit named Fear. It wants to torment you just like all of the other demonic spirits. Jesus cast spirits out of people in the New Testament, and they were healed of specific diseases or physical sicknesses. Demons can affect the body in many ways. They can cause illnesses and manifest real symptoms. It is essential to know that as we go along, studying the Word of God. The Spirit of Fear is a demon that will cause you to have a reaction in your body. Fear causes you to have a fight or flight response. This sometimes is natural. Like when you are in a field, and you are walking along peacefully, and you are confronted by a lion that is licking his lips and wanting to eat you. You will experience a little thing called fear. It starts off small, can fill you, and take over if you allow it.

It is natural to have certain emotions like anger and fear. However, the Bible warns that if we give in to these demons then we will be sinning. Anger leads to wrath and being filled with evil. Worry leads to fear and a complete lack of faith in God, consumption, and possession of an evil Spirit. Like any demonic spirit, it wants to convince you to believe that it needs to be around. Then it wants you to sign a contract allowing it to have a room in your spiritual house. Once it moves in, it wants to torment you day and night until you give up and allow it to take over your actions and, eventually, your body for possession.

Fear comes from the enemy and in direct opposition to the Word of God. The enemy wants you to doubt the Word of God. The Bible says that you can be healed if you have faith without doubting Matthew 21:21-22,

> *"So Jesus answered and said to them, "Assuredly, I say to you, if you have faith and do not doubt, you will not only do what was done to the fig tree but also if you say to this mountain, 'Be removed and be cast into the sea,' it will be done. And whatever things you ask in prayer, believing, you will receive."*

If you pray and are not healed, then you may not have prayed with enough faith to overcome your doubt. It could also be that your atmosphere is not suitable for the Holy Spirit to operate freely. Jesus experienced this problem and couldn't do miracles in some places because of the lack of faith by the people (Matthew 13:58). As you can see, it is vital for us to change our atmosphere around us as well as keeping our minds focused on God.

I told you that I have been sunbathing, but I have been in worship. I picked out a bunch of songs a long time ago and made a playlist on YouTube. I labeled it "Christian worship." I got alone in my house in my room and locked the door. I put on headphones and started the music. It was not an accident that all of this happened; it is called making a plan. It is a strategic plan of warfare against the enemy. Worship is vital to your walk with the Lord and your fight against the enemy. Worship music was played in the Old Testament before they went out to battle (2 Chronicles 20:21).

I knew a guy in his early 30's that was trying Buddhism and was very serious about it. He was diligent about it for weeks. One day after he saw me reading the Bible and worshiping, he started complaining about Buddhism. Buddhism teaches you to empty your mind and your soul. He said, "This religion is not working for me; all I am doing is emptying myself, but the problem is that I am empty." Wow. I was shocked at the revelation that God was showing him. As a non-believer, he knew that being empty or having a void was not right. He was empty, and he just wanted to be filled instead. I told him about Christianity and witnessed to him about Jesus. Unfortunately, he decided not to allow Jesus to save him. He rejected Jesus, and it was sad. People know that Jesus is the best thing for them, but they choose themselves instead of God, which can bring them Joy, Love, and Peace. He fills us to overflowing, and it is fantastic! Real Joy comes from the Lord and is a Fruit of the Spirit (Galatians 5:22).

You might be wondering why I am talking about worship so much when this chapter is supposed to be about fear. You must believe me that I am drunk in the Spirit. Yes, you are right. However, the Holy Spirit has me do this to remind you that it is best to stop everything and call on Jesus when you are going through hell. Jesus is the Prince of Peace! He will stop the storm in your life if you allow Him the opportunity. However, He will let the enemy attack us, but He is listening closely to us for just an utterance of His Name. Jesus is ready like a lifeguard to save you from going to hell and from the enemy when you are a Christian. Nevertheless, He is a Gentleman. He will not fight your battles for you. He has given you a voice. You can use it to call on Him and to fight against the enemy. Jesus calmed the storm on the boat when the disciples woke him up Mark 4:35-41,

> "On the same day, when evening had come, He said to them, "Let us cross over to the other side." Now when they had left the multitude, they took Him along in the boat as He was. And other little boats were also with Him. And a great windstorm arose, and the waves beat into the boat so that it was already filling. But He was in the stern, asleep on a pillow. And they awoke Him and said to Him, "Teacher, do you not care that we are perishing? Then He arose and rebuked the wind and said to the sea, "Peace, be still!" And the wind ceased, and there was a great calm. But He said to them, "Why are you so fearful? How is it that you have no faith?" And they feared exceedingly, and said to one another, "Who can this be, that even the wind and the sea obey Him!"

Jesus had a unique reaction when He woke up. You would think that Jesus would wake up, get frightened, and start bailing water out of the boat, right? NO! Jesus did not allow the things of this World to rob Him of His Peace. Jesus had declared just a few verses earlier, "Let us cross over to the other side!" Therefore, once He said something, He rested. This is how God operates. He declares and rests. His Word does the rest. We have to believe the Word of God and rest. True faith, once expressed and communicated, rests in God and does not worry about the results.

The disciples woke Him up and said, don't you care that we are going to die? The disciples were in complete panic and fear for their lives. This is a logical response to an event trying to take your life. He woke up and rebuked the wind. He then said to the sea, "Peace be still." After Jesus spoke, there was a great calm. After He spoke and fixed everything, He had some more things to say. He asked them why are you so fearful and how is it that you have no faith? Jesus is asking you these same questions today. You must answer Him in order to be set free. Ask yourself these questions and right down the answers until you have gotten to the root of the fear. For the disciples these were rhetorical questions because Jesus already knew the answer. However, the Bible says that they feared exceedingly and asked each other who this person is because of His Power?

The Disciples did not have strong faith in Jesus. They knew that Jesus could do miraculous things, but they were not convinced that He was the Messiah. They were more spectators than they were players on the team. The disciples ran like cowards when Jesus was captured, and none of them stood up with boldness. They did not understand the revelation of how to serve Jesus or who He was. The disciples did not get courage until the Holy Spirit filled them once Jesus gave the Holy Spirit (Acts 4:31). Afterward, the disciples were described as men of boldness and preached everywhere, regardless of the danger. They were beaten, jailed, and killed for their faith. There is a difference when someone is filled with the Spirit and with someone who is just being a spectator. This is the real difference between someone who has a close personal relationship with the Lord and someone who is just playing Church or being religious, which we will get into the next chapter.

Doubt kills faith. You have to decide who Jesus is to you. Jesus asked all of His disciples whom they thought He was (Matthew 16:13). They all had different answers or different perspectives of who He was. How you view Jesus is how you will have victory. The Word of God describes Jesus as the Son of

God with Authority over the enemy. Jesus had Authority over a thousand demons (Legion) and cast them out with no problem. He refused Satan and sent Him packing! He gave His Life on the cross for sin and victoriously rose from the dead. Jesus is the Lion of the Tribe of Judah, and every knee shall bow and confess that He is Lord. The demons yelled in fear and declared Him Lord while begging Him not to throw them into the pit of hell. Jesus has given us the Keys to the Kingdom, and given us authority over the enemy using His Name. We must only have faith in Him and His Word.

Doubting the Word of God will cause you to have anxiety. If there is no Absolute Truth you are trusting in then there is nothing that will save you. The Lord is real, but the enemy tries to make you think that He is not real or deaf and can't or won't hear your prayers. It may appear that God is asleep, but He wants you to exercise your faith. He wants you to decide who He is to you. If He is God and the enemy is no match for Him, then you believe in a God that is Powerful. If you believe that He gave you Power over the enemy, then you believe in that Power and not yourself or your abilities. If you believe this, then you will say to that mountain be removed, and it will jump into the sea. If you doubt, then you will be crushed by the mountain. James 1:7-8 says a double-minded man is unstable, "*For let not that man suppose that he will receive anything from the Lord; he is a double-minded man, unstable in all his ways.*" A person who cannot make up his mind is always confused. YOU MUST DECIDE! There is no middle ground in this fight.

Unstable in all of his ways is just the beginning. If someone is double-minded, then they have mixed feelings. Everything they do is in direct contradiction to the other belief that they have. They are confused according to James 1:5-7,

> "*If any of you lacks wisdom, let him ask of God, who gives to all liberally and without reproach, and it will be given to him. But let him ask in faith, with no doubting, for he who doubts is like a wave of the sea driven and tossed by the wind. For let, not that man suppose that he will receive anything from the Lord; he is a double-minded man, unstable in all his ways.*"

So, asking in faith without doubting is how to receive from the Lord, as seen in verse 6. However, he who doubts is just tossed around endlessly without mercy by any wind of Doctrine that blows. Let that person know that he will not receive anything from the Lord. Therefore, God is big on faith and against doubt. The Bible has spoken. Any Doctrine of Demons will toss us around and confuse or deceive us. The only way out is to have absolute faith in the Word of God. Faith in Religion will not do it. Faith in your Church or your Pastor will not do it. Faith in your friends or things will not do it. You must have faith in God.

Doubt in God's Word brings anxiety. Anxiety leads to panic and fear. If you do not have something to trust in, then you have no anchor or rock to stand on. God is our source of stability and faith. He gives us Peace Philippians 4:7 says,

"Be anxious for nothing, but in everything by prayer and supplication, with thanksgiving, let your requests be made known to God; and the peace of God, which surpasses all understanding, will guard your hearts and minds through Christ Jesus."

This is a powerful Scripture because the keys to breaking fear are here. Do you see them? Be anxious for nothing. How? In prayer is the answer. We are to ask God with supplications and petitions. This means to use our faith in God's Word and quote Scripture to Him in prayer about His Promises. Use faith in His Word to ask Him by faith to answer us in faith! Got it? Then with thanksgiving, we thank Him by faith for doing it!

So, it takes faith to pray, believing in faith in the Scriptures, and using them in faith to ask Him by faith for our requests, then petitioning Him by faith believing He will do it. Finally by faith, resting and thanking Him in faith that He will do it! Therefore, in summary, it is all by faith! Doubt has no part in faith. This type of faith will release the Peace of God that surpasses all understanding or any experiences you have had before. You will have so much Peace that you will feel drunk or relaxed. It is different from any feeling that drugs, alcohol, or anything this World can offer. This Peace is supernatural.

A pill cannot manufacture Supernatural Peace for anxiety. I am not telling you to stop taking your medication you are taking for anxiety if you are. However, I am telling you that if you practice this type of prayer as a lifestyle, you can have Peace anytime you need it. This is a Supernatural Peace, the kind that Jesus speaks, "Peace be still" to the sea in your life. The sea of emotions will come to a dead calm when this Peace surrounds and guards your heart. This Peace will guard your heart and minds. This is a promise that Jesus gives us. When we have faith in His Word and Him, then we will have this Peace. It will guard our hearts and minds. Jesus encourages us to drop the training wheels and walk on water. Walking in faith excites and pleases God.

The Holy Spirit is strong, and He will guard our minds against the oppression of the enemy. We have to make sure to have faith in God and surrender to Him daily and hourly if you understand what I am saying. The enemy does not stop trying to harass us, so we cannot stop seeking God to make sure He is flooding our hearts and minds with His Peace. It's not about Religion anymore for Christians today. The enemy is attacking Christians harder because his time is short, and the end times are upon us. It won't be tomorrow, but depending on when you are reading this book, it could be. We have to surrender to the Lord so He can save us from the enemy, but it is our responsibility to fight the enemy and not to fall into sin. Choosing to fear is a sin. If the Bible tells you to do something and you don't, then it is a sin. The Bible repeatedly says to have faith in God and trust the Word of God.

Anxiety and worry are symptoms of fear. If you catch yourself worrying about something, then you have to give it to the Lord. If you are going to worry, then you can't pray. If you are going to pray, then you can't worry. You have to decide who you are going to trust with your life past, present, and future. It all starts with a thought. You visit a doctor and get lab work done and they tell you they will call you next week. So, all week long, you can worry and stress about it or you can just trust God for the results. If you go to the doctor and the results are normal, then you wasted time worrying, didn't you? Now, if you go to the doctor and have high blood pressure, you can get on medication. However, you do not have to be in fear that you will have to deal with it your whole life. You can get in better shape and lose weight in the natural, but also pray to be healed in the supernatural. God wants us to take care of our temples. Our temple is where He dwells, so let's take care of it.

If you are experiencing fear and torment, then you are past a normal worry or concern. This is a long-term choice to worry and doubt the Word of God. When I say, doubt I mean not believe that it is untrue but that it doesn't apply to you. You may also be limited by your Religion. That's unfortunate! The Word of God is not a Religion. It is not limited by Religion. Religion puts limits on the Word, and this is demonic. Nothing can make the Word of God ineffective except you. What? Yup! If the Word of God says something, then It is true whether you believe It or not. If you doubt Scripture, then you doubt God. Read the Scriptures to get understanding and faith, and you will be amazed!

Fear is the opposite of faith. If you are full of faith and the Presence of God, then you cannot fear. The Bible says in 1 John 4:18, "*There is no fear in love; but perfect love casts out fear because fear involves torment. But he who fears has not been made perfect in love.*" Perfect Love casts out fear! This is God's Holy Spirit protecting us from fear. If we are full of His Love, then we have no room for fear. Perfect Love casts out fear. It rebukes and chases off fear. Fear cannot exist in your temple with perfect Love because it ejects fear. We are to seek God and be filled with His Love, then rinse and repeat. The enemy will fight us, and we need to rebuke Him and quote Scripture and trust in God's Word to protect us and cast out all fear. Jesus used the Word of God against the Devil. We have to do the same thing if we don't want to be oppressed by the Devil and be defeated.

Christianity is a battle, and you are a Warrior in Christ. Jesus is strong, and He wants to defeat the enemy in your life. You simply have to allow Jesus to fight through you. You cannot fight the enemy on your own (In your own strength). God will use your faith and your mouth, but you have to choose to do it in God's Power. You can tell the Devil to leave or shut up, but without the Holy Spirit's Power, he will just keep at it until you are worn down, and he will run you over. James 4:7 is the key, "*Submit to God and resist the Devil and he will flee from you.*" It doesn't say just resist the Devil. You have to submit to God in every area of your life and walk with Him. Make sure He is the Lord of your life. As you submit to God and walk in His authority, you can resist the Devil, and He will flee from you. Putting on your Armor and using It is the key to defending yourself from the enemy and defeating Him.

Worry is a sin, and it can turn demonic quickly; we have to fight it. God says He knows the plans He has for you. Good plans. Use Google or the Bible Concordance and look up Scriptures on trust. Write them all out by hand and memorize them. The way to fight fear is by trusting God. In the book "The Three Little Pigs" there is a perfect example of what the Devil tries to do to us. He likes to huff and puff and threatens to blow your whole house down. If you open the door to fear, then he will come in, hogtie you, and take over. He can be overwhelmingly persuasive, so we have to be ready to fight and reject his threats. Fear also will try to deceive you subtly. Fear steals your confidence and faith. Don't freeze in fear. Rebuke it off you and out of your mind. Fear will keep you from reaching your next level with the Lord.

Do not be afraid of Jesus, Isaiah 41:10 says, "Fear not, for I am with you; Be not dismayed, for I am your God. I will strengthen you, Yes, I will help you, I will uphold you with My righteous right hand." There are 365 references in the Bible that tells us not to fear. That is one for every day or 365 for one day! If you are being bombarded by the enemy, then use all 365 Scriptures and make him choke on the Word of God until he decides to leave you alone! Yup! Force-feed him the Word until he vomits. Then feed him some more. You must understand the enemy will not give up on you if you have any uncertainty about letting him back into your life no matter what sin it is. Demons hate being kicked out of a body. They will claw, scream, kick, and fight to get back in (Matthew 12:43-45). However, they do get tired and will leave you if you are using God's Power because they can't fight that. They try, but they finally get the hint if you don't give up! Stay rested and healthy. It's hard to fight if you are tired, hungry, or out of faith! Go back to God in worship, prayer, and reading His Word to be filled with faith.

Worry is warned against in the Scripture. We are not to worry, Matthew 6:33-34 says, "*But seek first the kingdom of God and His righteousness, and all these things shall be added to you. Therefore, do not worry about tomorrow, for tomorrow will worry about its own things. Sufficient for the day is its own trouble.*" We are to seek first the Kingdom of God and His Righteousness. If we put God first in everything that we do, then God will take care of us. Tomorrow has not yet shown up. Today is the tomorrow you worried about yesterday, and you are still alive and well. Tomorrow will never get here because today is the day that God has given. Today is the day that we are to obey the Lord. Live this day free, as it is your last day on earth. If you have already died in your mind (Broke the Contract of Fear), then the Devil can't scare you into being worried about every new sickness you find on the internet.

Logic is a tool the enemy uses all the time. You have to be careful to reject logic in every form. Logic is one of the Devil's favorite weapons. You cannot defeat the Devil with logic. You have to use the Word of God and have faith. Logic will deceive you into believing there is no hope. Phrases like "Well it happens to everyone," "You can't live forever," "God doesn't heal these days," and "That's why you have insurance," rob you of faith. Jesus said my sheep know My Voice. His Voice is encouraging. The Holy Spirit is gentle and not condemning. God will convict you but not yell or condemn you.

When I was a young Pastor, God told me, "You can't fight with the flesh." I immediately knew that God was talking to me directly. I tried to resist Satan constantly in many areas of my life. I was not submitting fully to God to get the victory. I was simply trying to fight by my own will and trying to be a better Christian by just saying no to sin. That is not how it works. The Bible says we have to walk in the Spirit in Galatians 5:16, "*I say then: Walk in the Spirit, and you shall not fulfill the lust of the flesh.*" When we are in the Spirit, we are content, and the Spirit is controlling the flesh. This is the only way to tame the flesh. It is unruly and wants to collect every demon spirit it can find. The flesh is almost as big of a problem as the enemy because they are friends.

Nevertheless, we will be victorious if we let God win the battle for us. Rejoice, and again, I say rejoice! Jesus has overcome the enemy! God hasn't given you a Spirit of fear 2 Timothy 1:7 says, "*For God has not given us a spirit of fear, but of power and of love and of a sound mind.*" We can have a sound mind if we allow God to fill us. Power is available through prayer and the Authority God has given us as Christians to use His Name. We need to rebuke the enemy continually with Power through the Spirit. Fear can bring depression because it makes you think that there is no hope. Hope deferred makes the heart sick (Proverbs 13:12) and can lead to depression or anxiety. We have to fight, so the enemy does not cripple us and leave us not wanting to get out of bed or losing relationships and jobs. It all starts with the first thought of the day. Start fighting at the beginning of the day, or you will be defeated by the end of the day. Let Love cast out fear, starting with your first thought of the day.

When the enemy gets us to fear something, then an evil spirit will come and torment us. Fear can cause your heart rate to be elevated, your mind to start racing, and even adrenaline to flow through your body. It can even invoke a fight or flight response in your body. We must always choose to fight fear with faith. God has given you a Spirit of Power to overcome the enemy. We must rebuke the enemy and use the Word of God against him. This will empower us and fill us with the Holy Ghost and faith. Sometimes when we are fighting the enemy, we will not feel energized by the Holy Spirit, but that does not mean that God is not flowing through us. There may be times we don't feel God at all and were just rebuking the enemy a bunch, but God is standing by watching our faith grow and is proud of us.

There are times to pray with other people, and there are times to pray by ourselves. There are times when people rebuke the enemy off of us, and there are times when we rebuke the enemy ourselves. We should be rebuking the enemy all day long every time he tries to put a thought in our head or threaten us. We should fight no matter what mood we are experiencing. We are to rest in the Lord. We can't rest if our heart is beating out of our chest or we are panicking. It's ok to stop and close your eyes and take a few deep breaths. This calms down your body and lowers your blood pressure and pulse. Then our body is calm, and we must take control of our mind by praying.

Surrender to the Lord and take all of your thought's captive. Your mind and spirit will be calm and empowered. Always choose to fight. When you stop fighting, the Devil will take you captive. Allow the Lord to show you that you are a warrior, and He will do it one battle at a time. Never be afraid of the enemy because Jesus has already defeated him. Emotions are created mainly by thoughts. If you control your thoughts, then your emotions will rarely get out of control. Take your thoughts captive and rebuke the enemy.

It is time to make a list to identify all of our fears. List out all of your fears and get them out of your head and on paper. This may take a while. You need to think about all of your anxieties and fears. What do you worry about during the day? What makes you lose sleep at night? Therefore, you need to ask yourself what your biggest fear is. How long have you had it? Where did it come from? Therefore, my question to you is, why fear? Why do you let fear wreak havoc on your life? Think about it. When did you first start to experience fear and anxiety? Did your parents deal with fear? Is it generational? You need to ask these questions and pray and ask God to show you when you first feared something unhealthy. Was it the fear of man? Fear of being alone? Fear of closed spaces? Fear of heights? What is your fear? Is it fear of failure? Fear of losing something or someone? When did the Devil deceive you into accepting fear? List out all your fears. I have made an outline in the back of the book to help you before you pray. Complete it and let's pray!

Now that you have a list of your fears and acknowledge them, it is time to surrender your fears to the Lord. Now, this requires you to give up on worrying. This requires you to start trusting the Lord to handle these problems. Do you think Jesus loves you? Do you think Jesus is bigger than your problems? Do you think Jesus knows how to take care of you? Ok, let us pray. Repeat this prayer out loud, "Father, I come to You today by faith. I believe the Word of God is real. I believe that no matter how I feel, Your Word is the Truth. I ask for Your Forgiveness for walking in fear and not trusting You. Forgive me for trying to do Your Job. I am not equipped to handle all of these problems. I need Your help, Lord. I trust You to take care of me. I place my life in Your Hands. I trust You. I know You love me. I renounce the spirit of fear. I renounce all evil spirits trying to control me. I accept You, Jesus, into my life. I receive Your Power. Holy Spirit please fill me, Lord please wash me clean. Help me to trust You. I make You Lord of my Life. I accept Your Peace. I rest in Your Finished Work. Help me to follow You and to trust You. Help me to fight the enemy daily. Help me to use the Wisdom from the Scriptures. Fill me with Your Perfect Love that casts out all fear. I Break the Contract of Fear I have signed with the enemy! I renounce the spirit of fear. Leave my life and do not return! Holy Spirit please fill me with your Spirit of Power and Love. Help me to hear Your Voice and obey It, in Jesus Name I pray, Amen."

Rejoice, Jesus is the Prince of Peace. He has flooded your temple and will do it as often as you turn to Him. You will be tempted to fear and to worry but keep fighting the good fight of faith. Trust in the Lord and His Word. Every time the Devil tries to get you to think about the future or to worry about something you need to rebuke it. Do not allow the Devil to have a place to put his thoughts in your mind. You can have peace anytime you want it through prayer. Pray, rebuke the enemy, and worship the Lord. God does not want you to be in fear. Take courage and trust in Your Lord Jesus who is able to take care of you. When you listen to fear you decide to trust the Devil. When you listen to faith you decide to trust God. Trust God and be free!

CHAPTER 7

The Contract of Religion

"Like a dog that returns to his vomit is a fool who repeats his folly." Proverbs 26:11

Praise God. It is a great day to be serving the Lord. I am excited to expose the works of Satan. He steals our joy, peace, and ruins our lives. Religious Spirits are evil demonic spirits that convince people to be religious or perfect, and they oppose God. Religious spirits continuously distract us from a genuine relationship with God. They turn us into Pharisees, and it is demonic. Pharisees were the religious leaders of Jesus' time that followed the Law hypocritically. They acted like they were perfect but were evil inside. They were guided by religious spirits and hated Jesus. Religious spirits are judgmental, prideful, arrogant, evil, and works-based accusing spirits. These sprits suck the life out of any Christian they get around. They tempt us to get religious about serving God and make it about Religion instead of a genuine close relationship with God. I will be discussing more about them and fighting them, but first, we must see how they speak to us and try to oppress us with their ways.

Religious spirits are very deceiving, and they bring with them other spirits as well. They do not work alone. This spirit wants to create a mindset in you that judges other Christians and their walk. It wants to get you in the habit of doing religious activities instead of having a close walk with the Lord. Let's look at the Scriptures to see how they operate to distract people from truly serving the Lord. Luke 10:38-42 says,

"Now it happened as they went that He entered a certain village, and a certain woman named Martha welcomed Him into her house. And she had a sister called Mary, who also sat at Jesus' feet and heard His Word. But Martha was distracted with much serving, and she approached Him and said, "Lord, do You not care that my sister has left me to serve alone? Therefore, tell her to help me." And Jesus answered and said to her, "Martha, Martha, you are worried and troubled about many things. But one thing is needed, and Mary has chosen that good part, which will not be taken away from her."

Martha was complaining that Mary was worshiping Jesus and not doing work. Jesus corrected her by saying, Martha, Martha, one thing is needed. Martha was trying to make the house and everything perfect. I'm sure she dusted and did everything she could. Martha had the Creator of this Universe in her home right in front of her, and she chose to do things to impress Him. Jesus let her know that this is not what He wants.

Jesus expects us to do the right thing and have integrity, but He wants obedience and not sacrifice when it comes to spiritual matters. The sacrifice is complete in Christ Jesus. He wants us to worship Him and get to know Him above anything else. When Jesus is at your home, He wants to spend quality time with you and not have you cater to Him. Most people are afraid of intimacy, so they do not surrender to God in worship. The goal of religious spirits are to make sure we do not truly worship God. They do not want us to enter into the Holy of Holies behind the Veil. They do not want us to apply the Word of God while repenting or have a daily visitation with God that will change us. When we spend time with God, we understand that He is a Loving God full of Grace and Mercy. We love to get this from God, but the demonic spirits don't want us to receive it or give it to others.

Religious spirits are taskmasters that want to punish people for not serving God correctly, according to the Law. Don't do this, and don't do that, this is what Religion is all about. Do's and don'ts are not what Jesus prioritizes as a genuine relationship with God (Not Religion). They want us to keep all of the Devil's Contract active. They want us to remain in sin while telling us we are doing a great job working with the Lord. Then they want us to judge others and gloat over them while never truly flowing in the Love of God. When we are full of the Spirit we have mercy and grace flowing in and out of our temples. We all know if we sin, then there is punishment for our sin. We know when we make a terrible decision that it is sinful. We can't ever stop sinning on our own. We need to walk in the Spirit to avoid fulfilling the evil desires of the flesh. Religious spirits try to force us to walk the Christian walk in our strength without help from God.

Let's look at the Temple in the Old Testament to see a clear picture (Exodus 25-30, 35-40). The Tabernacle of Moses has three parts. The layout of the Temple starts with a vast area around it called the Outer Court. It had a gate that leads into the Outer Court, which has the ritual Purification Basin and an Altar. Inside the Temple is the Holy Place it houses the Menorah on the Golden Lampstand, Table of Showbread, and Altar of Incense. Finally, there is the Holy of Holies, which has the Ark of the Covenant with the Mercy Seat on top of it as a covering. In the Holy of Holies is the place where God has designated the High Priest to experience His Direct Presence.

The High Priest had the duty of serving the Lord by performing all of the rituals to gain access to the Lord's Presence to atone for the sins of the people. Serving the Lord was serious because the Lord is Holy and has to judge sin with blood atonement. The High Priest had to perform many rituals, which are complex and very detailed. If he did not perform them correctly, then the Lord would kill Him for being disobedient. The High Priest in the Outer Court outside the Temple had to purify his hands and feet three times before he could even begin making sacrifices on the Altar. But before he started this purification ritual, He had to make sure he was wearing the right garments designed by God. They had to be formed correctly to His specifications. Once the High Priest had all of the correct garments and a gold plate on his head that read "Holy unto God," they would be able to start the rituals. He would be set apart for service wearing the right garments.

The High Priest would be in the correct garments, and then he could get started heading toward God's Presence. He started the ritual purification of washing his hands and feet and then making the temporary atonement or blood sacrifice. Then the blood would be applied to the Altar and other places strategically. He would then take the blood into the Holy Place or Inner Court and apply it to the Altar of Incense. He would burn incense as he lights the Menorah on the Lampstand. Once all of these rituals were correctly completed, then he could go past the covering of a thick Veil into the Holy of Holies. He would apply blood to the Mercy Seat seven times to atone for sins. This is a summary of how the Lord wanted the High Priest to atone for sins and the rituals involved.

When Jesus came to the Earth, He lived a sinless life and was sent by God to be atonement for sin, for all of humanity once and for all. Jesus was called the Lamb of God, who takes away the sin of the World. Jesus shed His Blood, and it was poured out seven places. Once while being beaten with a cat of nine tails, nails through each of His Hands and feet, plucking out His Beard, punching Him, sweating blood in prayer, having a crown of thorns on His Head and a spear through His Side. He died on the cross, and His blood directly made permanent atonement that was acceptable to God. Jesus was our High Priest because He atoned for the sins of all of humanity. He was the Creator of the World but had to atone for the sins of humanity Himself. God designed this whole thing, but rest assured whether you understand it or not it has happened. When Jesus died, the Veil leading into the Holy of Holies was torn from top to bottom. God showed the World that the sacrifices were no longer required or acceptable. Anyone can have access to the Presence of God through Jesus. Hebrews 10:19-22 says,

"Therefore, brethren, having boldness to enter the Holiest by the blood of Jesus, by a new and living way which He consecrated for us, through the veil, that is, His flesh, and having a High Priest over the house of God, let us draw near with a true heart in full assurance of faith, having our hearts sprinkled from an evil conscience and our bodies washed with pure water."

Jesus died for sin and went to God and made a path for us to reach God. The requirement to reach God is not based on rituals and sacrifices any longer because Jesus fulfilled the Law of Requirements for atoning for sin. Now the way to get to God is by believing in Jesus as the Blood Sacrifice. This atonement should not be replicated any longer by anyone else. Jesus has set down at the Right Hand of the Father and is making intercession for us now. He has the direct Ear of God, and those that believe and accept Jesus as Savior also have this access. Everything has changed from the Old Testament rituals, as described above. The path to God is through praying in Jesus Name. If you accept Jesus, then your sins have been atoned for, and you have received this forgiveness.

The Word of God explains that God is a loving God full of Grace. He calls us priests and gives us new responsibilities to serve Him without the need for atonement and purification to please God. God says that without faith, it is impossible to please Him. We now are to use faith as a key principle in everything that we do. Faith unlocks everything in the Kingdom of God. It is by faith in what Jesus has done and what His Word promises to us. God is longing for a personal relationship with us because He calls us the Temple of God. The old way of getting to God is cursed and demonic. When you try to seek God through ritualistic means of righteousness, then it is a trap by Satan. You see, satanic people sacrificing and using blood, but it is all demonic.

Many people try to earn their salvation or God's approval by doing things correctly (trying to be perfect). The Bible says that if you are perfect but break the Law of God in one tiny area, then you are guilty of all of the Law. Either you are perfect (which is impossible), or you are guilty of being a sinner. Perfection is a massive burden that no one can fulfill. Many have tried, and all have failed. God not only had laws about outward standards but inward laws as well. Jesus said that if you look at a woman to lust, you have already committed adultery without going through with the act. Sin starts in our mind before the actual breaking of the Law outwardly. God looks at our hearts and our thoughts. He knows us based on our inward person and not only by the things that we do outwardly.

God gives grace 1 Peter 5:5, "*Likewise you younger people, submit yourselves to your elders. Yes, all of you be submissive to one another, and be clothed with humility, for "God resists the proud, but gives grace to the humble."* We have to be humble and accept the Grace of God. We cannot be perfect; even the priests in the Old Testament couldn't be perfect. The High Priest was a sinner and he followed the prescribed way to cleanse himself by wearing the correct garments and washing his hands and feet. There has never been any perfect human, but the Devil wants us to think that we can be the first. Not only does he want us to think that we can be perfect but that it will actually impress God if we were. What a joke! We are sinners saved by Grace Ephesians 2:8-9, "*For by grace you have been saved through faith, and that not of yourselves; it is the gift of God, not of works, lest anyone should boast.*" It is by the Grace of God dying for us and our faith in that Gift that we are saved, and it is not by anything we can do because no one ever could. Jesus did it, and it is final. When He died on the cross, He said, "It is finished" (John 19:30).

Jesus paid the penalty of sin. He has freed us from rituals which the Bible calls dead works. Here is some meat for you to chew on Hebrews 6:1, "_Therefore let us leave the elementary doctrine of Christ and go on to maturity, not laying again a foundation of repentance from dead works and of faith toward God._" These religious actions are referred to by Paul as Elementary. We should move on and stop trying to be the perfect High Priest that atones for sin. Religious perfection is demonic and makes us think that we can be Jesus in our sinful flesh. We are not, and it is impossible to please God through our actions alone. You are offending the Lord and playing into the trap of the enemy. Paul asks rhetorically how can we begin by God cleansing us in the Spirit (Getting Saved) and we try to continue cleansing ourselves through the flesh (Works) in Galatians 3:3, "_Are you so foolish? Having begun in the Spirit, are you now being made perfect by the flesh?_" It is impossible for our actions through the flesh by perfection to add to what God did Spiritually through Jesus and the Holy Spirit.

The Devil has you in a loop of staying in the Outer Court and never reaching the Holy of Holies. You are constantly in sin and trying to purify yourself. You might go without sin and purify yourself by asking God for forgiveness but then trying to go through the Holy Place and perform the ritual of perfection to enter into the Holy of Holies. This whole process has been fulfilled, and it is demonic to keep trying this old, outdated religious way to please God. He tore the Veil in Solomon's Temple, and this all ended. The Veil that separated us from God was supernaturally torn by God from top to bottom as proof He did it, and the atonement is complete (Mark 15:38). Jesus even prophesied about the Temple's destruction, which happened in 70 A.D. The Temple has never been rebuilt since that time. That old way has passed, so surrender to the new way in Hebrews 4:14-16,

> "_Seeing then that we have a great High Priest who has passed through the heavens, Jesus the Son of God, let us hold fast our confession. For we do not have a High Priest who cannot sympathize with our weaknesses but was in all points tempted as we are, yet without sin. Let us therefore come boldly to the throne of grace that we may obtain mercy and find grace to help in time of need._"

Religious spirits influence people to serve God and not to spend time with Him. They get people to stay busy trying to please God with their efforts and not relax in God's Grace. When I say relax, I mean to rest in what Jesus has done. But rest assured knowing that the sin problem has been taken care of, and now it is time to move on to a genuine relationship with God. When we spend time with God, He shows us that we have a purpose and calling. He wants us to do things for Him but not in trying to be perfect to impress Him. We show him our devotion by doing His Will. This, of course, is by not committing sin, but it goes beyond that now. He wants us to serve Him by Grace.

He has given the Gifts of the Spirit and the Armor of God by which we serve Him in Love. This requires an infilling of His Love in our temples. We can try to do good things for God, but it winds up being empty and fruitless without His Power. Sure, things get done, but as Jesus said, "The poor you will have with you always." You must do His Will, not just good things in your effort. Doing things in your own power is like a person who is trying to pole vault without a pole. Without the pole, they will jump, and it will not be impressive, but with the pole, they will fly way higher and with minimal effort. This involves having a personal relationship with God. God will tell you what He wants you to do and confirm it through the Holy Spirit, which also resides within you. Jesus said, "My sheep know My Voice."

Now having seen a perfect way, let us, therefore, leave dead works and serve God through the intimacy of the Spirit. The way to do this is by spending time with God in His Presence. We must abandon sin to do this. We have to repent from our sin, which keeps us from the Presence of God. When we give up our idols, then that is how we purify ourselves through obedience. This obedience is not outwardly with do's and don'ts. It is an inward decision that God blesses with His Power to overcome sin, which controls our outward actions. If we are filled with the Spirit, we will not fulfill the lust of the flesh. Therefore, let us walk in the Spirit!

Religious spirits do not want you to walk in this freedom. They want you to sin and only to confess the sin but focus on doing better next time. They want you to confess to God, so you feel cleansed, but they want to keep you in the trap of arrogance, thinking that you can stop sinning or serve God in the flesh's power. When the contract has nothing but torment day after day, the contract will make you miserable. You are chained to the contract even if you don't understand all of the ramifications of what religious spirits do to you.

This is what the Pharisees did, and Jesus called them sons of Satan. Well, He said their father was the Devil, so that's the same thing. They were considered above reproach because they kept all of the Law to perfection (outwardly). Jesus was not impressed. He said inwardly they were ravenous wolves and wolves in sheep's clothing. Looking like the real thing, but inside they were evil to the core. You can be a fan of a sports team and know everything about them. This does not make you intimate friends with the coach. You can be a fan of Jesus and know the Bible really well. You can repeat facts and even teach other people but never have an intimate relationship with Jesus. It only makes you religious, and you have to get past knowledge into a genuine relationship with God.

The Pharisees and Sadducees repeatedly tried to trap Jesus in everything that He did or said (Mark 12:13-37). When religious spirits take over a person, they can't help but point out other people's sins. They like to point out that they are better than them and Lord it over them. This is a spirit of accusation and judgment that accompanies the religious spirit. These spirits try to trick Christians and accuse them. These spirits are evil and want to shame you into feeling condemned. They do seem to be genuine until you judge their fruit. They turn out to be jealous and miserable because misery loves company, and they try to drag you down with them. These demons are very discouraging and oppressive. They are works and knowledge based. They do not care about you and try to get you offended. Making you feel like you don't measure up to God's Standard. They want you to respond in the flesh and not the Spirit. Jesus always replied in the Spirit. He was patient because He knew what spirit in which they were operating. Sometimes it did not matter what answer He gave them; they would just get mad and try to put their hands on Him or kill Him.

These demonic spirits want to try to taunt you and debate with you until you slip up in one area with them, and then they point out your flaw. I remember dealing with a woman, and she had demons talking through her, and the demon kept slipping up and using third person terms when talking to me. You have to pay attention to what they say, but also how they say it. This is very important when using discernment. You must allow the Holy Spirit to show you if it is a demonic spirit or just a person. Either way, they are influenced by a religious Spirit. Pray for them and try to speak the Truth in love to them. If the Lord leads you ever to cast out a demon, make sure that you control that situation. Do not try to do it on an airplane or in a car. Make sure that you and preferably, someone with you can help you agree in faith and help cast the demons out.

If they do not want help, then you cannot argue with a person that has a demonic stronghold and win. Demons will eventually wear you down, and you will wind up getting offended. You cannot help someone who does not want help. You can go to them with another Christian and express your concern, but if they do not want to repent, it is best to pray for them and let God speak to them. You have to listen to the Lord, but unfortunately, with some spirits, it is a waste of time because the host has decided they want the demons to be there. This is sad, but it is a possible reality. If a demon has a stronghold in their life, then they will be fueled by demon logic and theology. You must not give into this because they try to make you feel crazy or outsmart you. They tried to do it to Jesus, but He had Divine Discernment and Power to deal with these foul spirits. You must be prayed up and ready to deal with them at all times.

Judgment Day will be full of people that hate God and want nothing to do with Him. They will suffer, but we can't rescue them or protect them from the Wrath of God. These spirits are always trying to push works and hate grace. They will try to push the Doctrine of losing your salvation. This is a works-based demonic belief. If you are saved, then you will want to serve the Lord. You may backslide, and it is wrong, but the Lord will correct you and allow you to repent. I have been there a few times. Let me tell you it is best not to backslide because the Lord carries a giant paddle and it hurts when He spanks His Children! Ouch.

We have to be on guard daily because we can backslide if we just keep listening to the enemy's voice in our heads. We have to fight and walk closely to the Lord to avoid sin and disobedience. Love covers a multitude of sins. Repent and do not judge others unless you are above reproach in that area Matthew 7:3-5 says,

"And why do you look at the speck in your brother's eye, but do not consider the plank in your own eye? Or how can you say to your brother, 'Let me remove the speck from your eye,' and look, a plank is in your own eye? Hypocrite! First, remove the plank from your own eye, and then you will see clearly to remove the speck from your brother's eye. "Do not give what is holy to the dogs; nor cast your pearls before swine, lest they trample them under their feet, and turn and tear you in pieces."

We have to make sure that we are not hypocrites in just pointing out someone's flaws or sins unless we are willing to repent ourselves. Jesus said repent first before you judge other people. This religious spirit will not admit fault or cause the person to look at their own sin. They feel self-righteous and do not remove the plank or massive piece of wood out of their eyes, which is blinding them from even seeing anything in front of them. They have to repent, and then they can see clearly to remove the speck from their brother's eye. We don't need to be on a fault-finding mission. Just check your motives. If you notice your speech is constantly degrading, judging others, telling others what to do, being hateful, or not speaking the truth with a loving spirit, you need to take a long hard look at why you are doing this. The Devil is called the accuser of the brethren, so why are you acting like him? Pray, and God will show you. The Holy Spirit will convict us of sin, so you don't need to do His Job. He wants you to restore the person in love and help the deceived person.

These religious spirits take over our minds and create a mindset in us that continually wants to compare our walk with someone else. Christianity is about loving people. If they are doing something sinful, then pray for them. If they will not repent, and it makes you mad, then you need to ask God why you are angry at their walk with God. Jesus warns us in verse 6 not to give what is holy to dogs or cast your pearls before swine. They will stomp all over your faith and tear you to pieces. If you see a person being religious, pray for them, and run away. It is a trap. If the Lord leads you to minister to them, then do it with wisdom and be prayed up. Take another person with you, and if they don't repent, then leave them alone.

Pray for them while shaking the dust off your feet. Matthew 10:14-17 says,

"And whoever will not receive you nor hear your words, when you depart from that house or city, shake off the dust from your feet. Assuredly, I say to you; it will be more tolerable for the land of Sodom and Gomorrah in the day of judgment than for that city! "Behold, I send you out as sheep in the midst of wolves. Therefore, be wise as serpents and harmless as doves. But beware of men, for they will deliver you up to councils and scourge you in their synagogues."

Either they are saved, and God will help them to repent, or they are not saved, and they are going to hell. Either way, they rejected the Word of God, and you need to pray and move on. You planted a seed, and God will water it. Just don't do it in a wrong spirit because it will cause that person to be more defensive and dig their heels in and fight you. In the past, I did all I could in the right Spirit and through prayer, but sometimes people don't respond.

You should be showing the Grace and Love of God toward someone who is caught in a sinful pattern Galatians 6:1, "*Brethren, if a man is overtaken in any sin, you who are spiritual restore such a one in a spirit of gentleness, considering yourself lest you also be tempted.*" This is convicting to us because the religious person does not care how bad their attitude is. We must not respond in the same way. We should have a Spirit of Gentleness when dealing with people caught in sin. Speak the Truth in love. It is a reminder of how we are to act as Christians. If you have been operating in any other way, then examine yourself. If what I have been speaking to you makes sense then you may have a spirit of Religion. There may be other spirits that have been tormenting you as well and it is time to Break the Devil's Contract.

Repeat this prayer, and let's allow the Love of God to fill our hearts and minds. "Heavenly Father, I need You in my life. I come to You asking for Your Help. I have not been walking close to You, and I repent of my sins. I need Your Grace in my life. I can't be a Christian without You. I give up trying to do it in my efforts. I need Your Love to wash over me. I renounce my evil ways and ask You to please forgive me. Help me to love people the way that You do. I renounce every demonic Spirit working in my life. I close the door to all demonic activity in Jesus Name. Help me, Lord, to serve You with a pure heart. Help me, Lord, to read Your Word every day and have an intimate relationship with You. I need more of You in my life, and I am asking You to soften my heart and help me hear Your Voice. I Break the Contract of Religion that I have made with the enemy. I renounce all of the spirits of self-righteousness, pride, and religion! Holy Spirit, I invite You in to fill me up with Your Spirit. Let me start today, walking in love. In Jesus Name, I pray, Amen!" Rejoice for the Spirit of the Lord is bringing freedom into your life. Let's move on to learn more about getting free in Jesus!

CHAPTER 8

The Contract of Lust

"I beseech you therefore, brethren, by the mercies of God, that you present your bodies a living sacrifice, holy, acceptable to God, which is your reasonable service. And do not be conformed to this world, but be transformed by the renewing of your mind, that you may prove what is that good and acceptable and perfect will of God." Romans 12:1-2

There is a war going on for your temple. The Devil wants to take complete control of it. He wants your mind and body. He wants your full devotion and worship. The Devil knows that he can get it from you as long as he keeps trying to wear you down. He will offer you all of the things that he thinks will cause you to sell out to him. With Jesus, he tried numerous tactics. He does the same to us, except we are more susceptible to him than Jesus. Jesus had the Holy Spirit without measure and was God in the flesh. We are not God, so we are capable of sin. We have to renew our minds daily to allow God to come in and stop Satan from taking over our lives.

Little did we know that when we got saved that we were in for a lifelong battle. I knew of a fight but did not realize that it was going to be this intense. The battle is serious, and whether we want to or not, we have to fight. We have been drafted into a war, and there is no going home after one tour. We have a daily fight on our hands. Some days we allow God to fight through us, and we are victorious. A majority of days for most Christians are filled with defeat. This defeat is a result of our free will. We decide to allow sin in our lives without repenting. An idol is defined as anything that we put between God and us. Idolatry is a huge problem. Today, we serve idols that are not Asherah Poles and Golden Calves, which are some of the Old Testament idols. We serve screens, ourselves, other people, things, and this culture.

Idolatry happens when we decide to sit on the throne or set something else on the throne. We remove God and then put ourselves on the throne or something else we want to serve. Lust is everywhere in our culture. People lust after images of perfection. People spend thousands of hours a year taking pictures and trying to perfect them to post online. It's all about self, and this culture promotes that. Image is a thing that is continuously changing and can never be obtained. It is vain to serve yourself and promote your image. This outward temple will fade, and we will all wither away until He comes. This culture encourages idols, and it is an evil culture. Christians in America are the only thing keeping evil from completely taking over as it has in other countries. In other countries, you cannot preach about Jesus without being jailed or killed.

We are in a country that resembles Sodom and Gomorrah. It was ripe for the Judgment of God. We are practicing idolatry, witchcraft, homosexuality, and have kicked God out of our everyday lives. This culture has gone down the tubes in the last 40 years that I have been alive. I remember watching T.V. growing up and there was no cursing and rarely saw women dressed inappropriately. On television these now, there is homosexuality, perversion, transgender, and many abominations that are spoken against in the Bible. Lust is a problem, and it's not just T.V. that has allowed it in. There is a whole World on the web that promotes it and makes billions a year doing it. The culture has relaxed now to accept anything, and we are not to bully anyone with our opinion or views. Bullying and shaming are new things that are considered evil.

Satan is a master of deception and manipulation. He slowly brings in evil things but places them in wholesome ideas. For instance, there is a good show that promotes family and has a few homosexual characters. The family embraces these people, and then the show makes them the favorites. They get more screen time, and the viewers accept their lifestyles. Let me make something clear. No matter what sin you have done in your life or are committing now, God loves you. He will forgive you and accept you if you repent from your sins and obey His Word. But to do this, we have to go back and break the entire Contract we have signed with Satan. Allowing the culture to influence us is an area that we have compromised in and formed a firm contract with the enemy. We have to change our hearts and minds and allow the Holy Spirit to convict us when we watch anything contrary to Biblical

Principles. I am not saying that you can't watch secular things. I am saying that many secular things are not healthy for your walk with God and are a distraction from you walking closely with God.

We live our lives the way that we want to, and then we blame God because we feel that He has left us. It's like Jesus on the cross when He said God, "Why have you forsaken me?" God had placed the entire sin of the World on Him. He judged Him, and where sin is, there cannot be light. Understand what I am telling you. Listen. If you have chosen to sin in a particular area, then that door is locked to God. He is not going to kick down the door. You have to allow Him to come in and clean up the room. It's like God comes in holding a trash bag, and you hand Him everything you want to throw away. He is not going to go in and start throwing everything away. Just letting Him stand at the door is not enough either. You have to let Him in to talk to you about your possessions. He has to come and talk with you and try to convince you that you need to clean your room. You might say, "It's my room; I don't need to clean it, and I am comfortable the way it is." This is just like a pig in filth, they are comfortable. A dog with fleas is another word picture that sticks in mind. They itch, are annoying, and are an infestation.

The spirit of lust is sneaky, and it comes with other demons as well. The spirit of perversion is its ugly cousin. These spirits are continually trying to break down your Biblical moral values until they can strike at your core beliefs. These demons want you to question everything God has ever said about sex and sexuality. The Bible says that we are not to lust or have sex outside of marriage. In the Bible, it was common to be a virgin until you were married. Today condoms are passed out to the students with the view that there is nothing we can do to stop it from happening because they will do it. These spirits have taken over America, and we as Christians have to fight back against evil. It is not a religious act I am talking about. People that are practicing the LGBT etc. lifestyle are people that Jesus loves. There is hope for them if they repent from their sin and accept Jesus as Lord. Christians can even get deceived into this lifestyle after they are saved, but they have the Holy Spirit telling them every day to repent.

We cannot make one sin worse than the other anymore. Sin is the result of the Devil getting into our lives and convincing us that sin is ok to do. The person sinning has been diluted and deceived by the enemy. We must preach the Word of God as Absolute Truth in this evil culture. It is ok to do anything that you want right now except preach against sin like sexual perversion. We are to love the sinner but not the sin. Christians, we must realize what we are wrestling against Ephesians 6:12 says, "*For we do not wrestle against flesh and blood, but against principalities, against powers, against the rulers of the darkness of this age, against spiritual hosts of wickedness in the heavenly places.*" We are wrestling against demonic spirits that have deceived people and influenced their thoughts and created a stronghold in their minds. It's a demonic lie that tells someone they can be a homosexual or transgender, and it's ok. We have to attack that lie and not the person. They are confused about their identity.

We are tasked with an unending job fighting the culture because it has affected everyone. We must first allow God to liberate us from this perversion. It's like the chicken and the egg when you talk about perversion and lust. Did our minds get perverted before we lusted, or did we lust at something, and then it perverted our minds after we sinned? We have to wake up and realize that this evil culture must be rejected by Christians. We cannot continue to serve God and have an intimate relationship with Him if we participate in this culture. Do you think I am too religious? If you do, then you still do not understand what I am trying to say to you. I love watching all kinds of different programming, but most of it is infested with this World's perversion. Once you watch it, it gets all over you, and the evil promoted in it gets stuck in your mind. Not only that, but almost all programming these days avoid talking about God. The T.V. or media is programming you to not think about God. It is called television programming. Anything you watch or do tries to program your mind. God knew this, and He said we should renew our minds daily with the Word of God.

We are affected by what we watch and hear daily. It reminds me of Slimer, one of the ghosts of "Ghostbusters." It appears silly and harmless, but when it comes after you, it slimes you leaving a thick goo that doesn't come off easily. That is why the Word of God says that we are to be transformed daily by the reading of the Word in Romans 12:2, "*And do not be conformed to this world but be transformed by the renewing of your mind, that you may prove what is that good and acceptable and perfect will of God.*" You saw this Scripture at the beginning of the chapter, but does it make sense yet? Do you see how you have been in sin this whole time just because you accept the culture? If the Bible says not to do something and then you do it, it is a sin. No matter how you try to justify it, the Bible is right, and you are wrong. The Truth hurts, but It will set you free if you know It and follow It closely. When someone is tired of being in bondage, they will escape by any means necessary. That is me while living in this evil World. I like many things it has to offer, but it almost always compromises my walk with God in one way or another. Let the Word of God be true, and every man a liar. We are to obey the Word of God not because it is the right thing to do "Martha Syndrome" or "Religious thing to do," but because it grieves the Holy Spirit and we want to serve God so we must not conform to this World.

The Word of God is showing you what the Holy Spirit is telling the Church. Romans 12:1-2,

> *"I beseech you therefore, brethren, by the mercies of God, that you present your bodies a living sacrifice, holy, acceptable to God, which is your reasonable service. And do not be conformed to this world, but be transformed by the renewing of your mind, that you may prove what is that good and acceptable and perfect will of God."*

I remember being taught these Scriptures in Bible College. When I got saved, I enrolled in Bible College within a few months. I read the Bible like crazy, but I remember the professor breaking down this passage, which helped me out so much. I will try to do this passage justice so you will have the same experience. We can find the perfect Will of God by obeying these Scriptures.

We talked a little bit before about the Old Testament Tabernacle with all of the rituals that had to be completed by the High Priest before he was allowed into the Holy Place or the Holy of Holies. Now the Altar of the Lord was where the sacrifices were to be presented and killed as atonement to the Lord. The animal was sacrificed, and its blood was used for rituals. Romans 12:1 says that we are living sacrifices, "*I beseech you therefore, brethren, by the mercies of God, that you present your bodies a living sacrifice, holy, acceptable to God, which is your reasonable service.*" The problem with living sacrifices is that when they are on the altar, they can slide off when it gets too uncomfortable. We are to present our bodies as a living sacrifice. Holy and acceptable is a requirement of a sacrifice in the Old Testament Leviticus 1:3, "*If the offering is a burnt offering from the herd, you are to offer a male without defect. You must present it at the entrance to the tent of meeting so that it will be acceptable to the Lord.*"

We are to present our bodies as a living sacrifice. This means a willing participant that is ready to go at any time. We are to be prepared at all times to be used by God in 2 Timothy 4:2, "*Preach the word! Be ready in season and out of season. Convince, rebuke, exhort, with all longsuffering and teaching."* So, we are to be ready to present ourselves as a living sacrifice without blemish that is acceptable to God, which is our reasonable service. This phrase reasonable service means that it is something that the Lord believes is a reasonable thing to ask of you to serve Him properly. Now you can see that the Lord requires us to serve Him and not simply be a believer. The Bible says that even demons believe in God and tremble, but they oppose God. We are called to action by the Lord without excuse. He wants us to serve Him. It is a tremendous privilege to be used by the Lord. I love serving God and allowing Him to use me. It is not easy to sacrifice my flesh to be in a close relationship with Him, but it gets easier. Once you tell your flesh no, it wants to rebel. But when you starve it out, then its voice will become a faint whisper. You will experience the Joy of the Lord, and It will energize you supernaturally. You won't miss your worldly, evil, fleshy desires being fulfilled, and the condemning voice of the enemy.

Conforming to this World is a sin in the eyes of the Lord, Romans 12:2 says, *"And do not be conformed to this world, but be transformed by the renewing of your mind, that you may prove what is that good and acceptable and perfect will of God."* So, we are told to be not conformed to this World, instead we are to be transformed by the renewing of your mind through the washing of the Word of God. This is a daily thing we should do because the enemy is trying to transform our minds daily through the ways of the World and its influences. God encourages us to be ready, so we can walk on water when He calls us to step out of the boat. If we keep looking down at the cares of this World, then we will keep falling, and Jesus will have to continually pull us out of the water. This cycle keeps on repeating when we are disobedient to the Word of God. The time for us to just do the bare minimum as a believer is over. The World is taking over, and we have to fight against evil forces.

The World is telling us that sex is ok outside of marriage, and it is ok to do whatever you want with whomever you want. This is a lie from the pit of hell. We are told to run from evil in 2 Timothy 2: 21-22,

> *"Therefore, if anyone cleanses himself from the latter, he will be a vessel for honor, sanctified, and useful for the master, prepared for every good work. Flee also youthful lusts; but pursue righteousness, faith, love, peace with those who call on the Lord out of a pure heart."*

We can be considered a vessel for honor and sanctified if we repent and serve God instead of sin. To conquer lust, we must pursue righteousness and seek God with all of our hearts. Lust is a desire that has been perverted by the enemy in our lives. Lust seeks to use and defile. The only way to get rid of this desire is to be filled with love. Love conquers lust and all evil desires. 1 John 1:9 says, "*If we confess our sins, he is faithful and just and will forgive us our sins and cleanse us from all unrighteousness.*" God can clean your mind from lust and perversion. You have to repent and believe in God's Word completely.

It should go without saying, but I will clarify some things that are not Biblical. Sex before marriage is not Biblical. Having a same-sex sexual relationship is not Biblical. Fornication, lusting, and masturbation are a sin. Watching porn and nudity, along with other sexually tempting things, are also sinful. Withholding yourself from your married partner is also a sin that is warned against strongly in 1 Corinthians 7:5, "*Do not deprive one another except with consent for a time, that you may give yourselves to fasting and prayer; and come together again so that Satan does not tempt you because of your lack of self-control.*" God gave you all that you need in your spouse, and you do not need anyone or anything else. Sex is a Holy thing in the sight of the Lord for married people. Sex is an intimate experience for married people, but the Devil wants to pervert it for everybody. The Devil wants sex to be a common thing that anybody can do at any time, and it means nothing. This bonds you to the flesh of the other person, which is demonic outside the confines of marriage Genesis 2:24 says, "*For this reason a man shall leave his father and his mother, and be joined to his wife; and they shall become one flesh.*"

The Bible says that you cannot play with fire without being burned Proverbs 6:27-29, "*Can a man take fire to his bosom, And his clothes not be burned? Can one walk on hot coals, And his feet not be seared? So, is he who goes into his neighbor's wife; Whoever touches her shall not be innocent?*" The fact is that if you are married, then you cannot cheat. If you are single, you cannot cheat either because that is someone else's future husband or wife. We are married to God, and if we get married to someone else, then we become one flesh with them but still married to God. Lust and perversion corrupt your mind and body. There are sexually transmitted diseases and all sorts of problems with sex outside of marriage. Lust wants you to obey its voice Romans 6:12-14,

"Therefore, do not let sin reign in your mortal body, that you should obey it in its lusts. Do not offer any part of yourself to sin as an instrument of wickedness, but rather offer yourselves to God as those who have been brought from death to life; and offer every part of yourself to him as an instrument of righteousness. For sin shall no longer be your master because you are not under the law, but under grace."

We should not offer ourselves to lust or the enemy. We should offer ourselves to God. Sin is no longer our master, and we do not have to obey it! Wow, this is an astonishing truth if you will hold onto it. We do not have to sin because sin is not our master any longer.

The Devil wants you to fall into the sin of lust. When you sin, you will want to do it again because sin is fun at first until the consequences start. When you give the Devil an open door, then he will start calling to you like a stray kitten that you gave food and milk to one time. It will keep coming back when it is hungry, and it will meow and meow until it annoys you to death. Instead of running the kitten off, you simply feed it again, so you don't have to hear it meow. Then it starts coming around more often, and you just keep feeding it. Then before you know it, you are spending a lot of time feeding this kitten until it becomes a cat. Finally, you just let it in the house and put out a big bowl of food and water for it in its own bowl that you went and bought for it. Now it is a permanent resident, and you are committed.

The sin of lust like others comes on so subtle and innocent, and you wind up, accepting it, and being trapped. This applies to sex before marriage, porn, and all sexual sin. The Devil wants to be your puppet master, and when he pulls strings you move. This spirit will oppress you and possess you if you allow it. You have got to put a stop to that evil spirit and get it out of your temple. You have to stop worshiping these demons. When we obey these demons then we are worshiping them and giving them our temple when they tempt us or tell us to. When the contract has nothing but torment day after day, the contract will make you miserable because you have to obey it. You are chained to the contract even though you didn't understand all of the ramifications of what lust does to you.

The Devil is crafty. He will have you meet someone, and then you slowly get to know them, and then you have sex. Because you have developed feelings for them as a person, you feel that you cannot cut off the relationship because you do not want to hurt their feelings. After all, you wanted to have sex and were selfish, so they shouldn't be punished, right? You both moved in together, and now you are saving money on the bills, so it is all a big blessing, right? But in your personal life, you stopped praying daily. You stopped reading the Word of God. You stopped going to Church. Then as you get to know them more, you realize you don't know if you want to get married for sure or not. Is this person right for me? Are they even a Christian (2 Corinthians. 6:14)? What did you get yourself into? How did this all happen? I don't feel close to God anymore. God, where did you go?

God did not go anywhere. What happened is you signed a Contract of Lust with the Devil. You allowed the Devil to come in and tempt you to sin. You stayed in that sin until you let it control you. You gave into the reasoning and logic of demonic spirits, and you were deceived by sin. You willingly sinned and thought that you were smarter than God and that you could get away with sin. You thought you could sin, and life would be better. You can sin and save money. Believing the lie that sin will help you is the worst thing you can do. Sin is a trap. We can become slaves to sin if we submit to it. It will control us and tell us what to do, and we will be powerless. But God can set us free from the power of sin. God is our Master, and He wants us to be free. Romans 6:15-18,

"What then? Shall we sin because we are not under the law but under grace? By no means! Don't you know that when you offer yourselves to someone as obedient slaves, you are slaves of the one you obey, whether you are slaves to sin, which leads to death, or to obedience, which leads to righteousness? But thanks be to God that, though you used to be slaves to sin, you have come to obey from your heart the pattern of teaching that has now claimed your allegiance. You have been set free from sin and have become slaves to righteousness."

We are no longer slaves to sin, but we are truly slaves to righteousness. This truth will set you free and allow you to live a life unto God. It's time to submit to the Word of God and cast off the sin that so easily traps us, Hebrews 12:1-2,

"Therefore, since we are surrounded by such a great cloud of witnesses, let us throw off everything that hinders and the sin that so easily entangles. And let

us run with perseverance the race marked out for us, fixing our eyes on Jesus, the pioneer and perfecter of faith."

We must stop turning to sin to satisfy us and allow God to fill us so we can run the race of freedom in Jesus. Sin separates us from God.

We have a relationship with God, but when we sin, we choose to serve it instead of God. It's not easy to just cast off sin if you have made it a habit to serve sin. We must keep our eyes on Jesus, so we don't allow the flesh to rule our lives. We have to pray that God will grant us repentance and come to our senses to escape the Devil's snare because we have been taken captive by him to do his evil will. We must have humility, surrender, and repent. It's our reasonable service. We must be ready to stand before God as a willing sacrifice. If you feel the Lord speaking to you, then choose this day whom you will serve. Let's pray and get the Devil out of our lives so God can set us free!

Repeat this prayer, "Heavenly Father, I ask that You would forgive me of my sins. I have been worldly and have not obeyed Your Word. My mind has been perverted. Lord please wash my mind from evil and lust. I renounce the Contract I have signed of Lust. I repent of lust and perversion. I break the Contract of Lust in Jesus Name. Lord, please deliver me from sexual sin. Help me to fall in love with You. Help me not to act out in lust and perversion and serve my flesh. I dedicate my temple to you in purity. Lord renew my mind and give me a pure heart. Purify me, Lord, so I can serve You. Help me to put You first. I need You in my life. Help me to have an intimate relationship with You. Fill me with Your Love. Wash me with Your Blood. In Jesus Name, I pray. Amen." Now that you have prayed and repented from lust and perversion it is time to fill this room with the Holy Spirit. Let's move on to learn how to be free from the enemies grasp and serve the Lord!

CHAPTER 9

The Contract of Condemnation

"There is therefore now no condemnation to those who are in Christ Jesus, who do not walk according to the flesh, but according to the Spirit." Romans 8:1

What a blessing it is to be free in Jesus today! To be able to access the direct Presence of God without hindrance is a blessing. To freely enjoy the Lord and receive blessings from Him is awesome. I am excited to talk with you about condemnation. I am excited that God will give you a revelation of condemnation, and the enemy will have to evacuate the place that he has in your life. Today the Contract of Condemnation is going to be broken. You will be one step closer to serving the Lord with all of your heart, mind, soul, and strength. Where the Spirit of the Lord is, there is freedom. Let's look at the Contract of Condemnation to see what deceptions the enemy has forced upon you.

Condemnation is defined as the expression of extreme disapproval, censure, or the action of condemning someone to a punishment or sentencing. We understand that condemnation is severe. God condemned sin Romans 8:3 says, "<u>For what the law could not do in that it was weak through the flesh, God did by sending His own Son in the likeness of sinful flesh, on account of sin: He condemned sin in the flesh.</u>" God is a Holy God. He cannot accept sin as an acceptable part of any reality. God is Holy, and in order for us to have a relationship with Him, we cannot have sin in that equation. God will not allow sin to be around Him and go unpunished. God hates sin so much that He sent Jesus to die to make atonement for it. Sin is evil in the sight of the Lord. Sin is a direct rebellion to God's Laws or Standards.

In math, we know that 1 plus 1 equal two; this is an Absolute Truth. Sin is a problem that only God can solve. He had a solution when the problem of sin presented itself. Now when we participate in sin, we fall under the Law of Sin and Death, according to Romans 8. The Law in the Old Testament was given to convict people of sin. The Law revealed the inability of people to keep it perfectly. What? Yes. The Law was given to show us that we could not follow it with perfection. The Law magnifies sin in our soul that wants to be loosed. The flesh is a fallen sin nature that resides within us, according to the Bible. The flesh is always looking for ways to be satisfied. We cannot go one day without the flesh trying to manipulate and control us into feeding it. Once the flesh has sin to eat, then it just gets hungrier. It's a problem that cannot be fixed by human methods or with human solutions. Your "Strong will" will not fix the issue of the flesh! We have to realize that we need a supernatural solution to sin and our sinful flesh.

The Book of Romans is full of Christian Doctrine, so it needs to be studied carefully. The Apostle Paul gives us a real glimpse into the problem of sin after being born again and walking with the Lord in Romans 7:15-20,

> *"What I don't understand about myself is that I decide one way, but then I act another, doing things I absolutely despise. So, if I can't be trusted to figure out what is best for myself and then do it, it becomes obvious that God's command is necessary. But I need something more! For if I know the law but still can't keep it, and if the power of sin within me keeps sabotaging my best intentions, I obviously need help! I realize that I don't have what it takes. I can will it, but I can't do it. I decide to do good, but I don't really do it; I decide not to do bad, but then I do it no matter what. My decisions, such as they are, don't result in actions. Something has gone wrong deep within me and gets the better of me every time."*

These Scriptures above are from the Message Bible, and it is explained in a specific way so we can understand it more straightforward. The New King James says it a different way, Romans 7:15-20 says,

> *"For what I am doing, I do not understand. For what I will to do, that I do not practice; but what I hate, that I do. If then, I do what I will not to do, I agree with the law that it is good. But now, it is no longer I who do it, but sin that dwells in me. For I know that in me (that is, in my flesh) nothing good dwells; for to will is present with me, but how to perform what is good I do not find. For the good that I will to do, I do not do; but the evil I will not to do, that I practice. Now if I do what I will not to do, it is no longer I who do it, but sin that dwells in me."*

We can see that sin is in our nature (Law of Sin and Death), and we cannot figure it out in order to beat it. The only way we can is to submit to the Lord and allow Him to fight sin through us by what Paul describes the Law of the Spirit of Life in Christ Jesus in Romans 8:2, "*For the law of the Spirit of life in Christ Jesus has made me free from the law of sin and death.*" Now the laws referred to here deal with the flesh and the Spirit within the Christian. The flesh leads us to sin, but the Spirit leads us to righteousness before God.

Our spirit cannot sin and be condemned, and our flesh (sin nature) cannot be sanctified. That is a loaded statement, but study it out thoroughly to get revelation from God. We will be saved because Jesus redeemed us and sealed us with the Holy Spirit. But our flesh (Sin nature) cannot be saved. It must be starved, put on a cross, rebuked, denied, and every other synonym you can find in the dictionary. We are not to cater to the flesh (Sin nature) it says this in Romans 13:11-14,

"And do this, knowing the time, that now it is high time to awake out of sleep; for now, our salvation is nearer than when we first believed. The night is far spent, the day is at hand. Therefore, let us cast off the works of darkness, and let us put on the armor of light. Let us walk properly, as in the day, not in revelry and drunkenness, not in lewdness and lust, not in strife and envy. But put on the Lord Jesus Christ, and make no provision for the flesh, to fulfill its lusts."

We are told not to make any provision for the flesh. Ok, so now we have a problem. You might be thinking, "I can't stop sinning, so I give up and want to start stocking up on what my flesh wants." You do this so you don't have to go shopping as much or be reminded to shop. NO! Defeated people think this way. We can defeat sin in our lives one day at a time and one temptation at a time. If you are all stocked up on sinful food for your flesh, you must throw it all out. You can win through Christ Jesus. The Devil wants us to give up and just give in to the pesky, horrible, shameful, wretched flesh that seems never to want to shut up. Well, Jesus has no problem overcoming your flesh if you just let Him. It takes a daily submitting to God and infilling with the Spirit. The Joy of the Lord will supernaturally choke out your flesh and leave it unconscious so that you can live in victory. The flesh will wake up to try to take control, but you have to choke it back out and put it to sleep (By God's Supernatural Power). Sing praise and worship songs to your flesh and put it to sleep!

The process of taking control of your flesh by the Spirit is called sanctification. This is learning how to walk with God so we can allow God to transform our minds with God's Word. The renewing of the mind helps us to renew our sinful way of thinking. You are reprogramming your mind to serve God in righteousness by obedience to Him and not by perfecting the Law or being perfect. Here is where the Devil likes to come in and confuse you and try to destroy any progress that you are making. You are serving the Lord and reading the Word, and here comes a person to tempt you. It can be that this person is attractive and loose in their morals, and they tempt you to sin. The

Holy Spirit knows the temptation is coming and warns you before and during the temptation. Once you give in to this sin, then you are obeying your flesh (Sin nature). Once sin is committed, you have grieved the Holy Spirit, and the enemy and sin have now come between you and God.

Just so you can understand this process, I will explain it in a way that makes sense. You have two Christians that are friends and love the Lord. They have been serving the Lord for the same amount of time and are being sanctified in their walk with God. They are saved, and that makes them justified (Saved) before God. Now because of loneliness or another reason, Steve gets tempted to take the friendship to another level. He gets impatient with the way that God wants him to do it, and he invites Jenny out on a date. Satan tempts Steve to want to break God's Law and sin. Steve gives in to the temptation, and so does Jenny and they have sex. So now they have both sinned. They have both disobeyed God's Law and now have a choice to make. Do they go on with their lives and pretend they didn't just break God's Law? Do they harden their hearts to the Voice of the Lord and keep sinning? Do they turn to God and repent for their sin? The way they handle this is essential.

If they pretend that they didn't break God's Law and keep sinning, this means they have committed to sin. They are choosing to disobey God continually and not even regard His Holy Law. They are grieving the Holy Spirit and are in sin. This sin separates them (Distances them) from God, and they are in disobedience (Rebellion toward God's laws). They have chosen to sin, worship one another, put themselves on the Throne of God, and set God to the side while doing their will. Now, this is a dangerous place for them to be. God does not condone rebellion and will not allow Christians to break His Law and get away with it. He chooses what He does to this couple as they continually sin and rebel from Him. They harden their hearts to the Voice of God and do not repent from their sin being worldly.

Many Religions teach that the people that fall into sin are now going to hell. Maybe they think this themselves, and they just give in to sin because they are damned. Now the Bible does not say this about someone in sin. We are to confess to the Lord and gently confront one another and repent. The Lord is full of Grace and is happy when we choose Him over sin. There may be consequences during our time of sin, but when we come back to Him, He is happy to meet us and accepts us gladly as Luke 15:20 says, "_And he arose and came to his father. But when he was still a great way off, his father saw him and had compassion, and ran and fell on his neck and kissed him._" The son realized that because of sin, he had a hard life. He would rather go back and be a servant than stay in sin. But when He comes to the father, he is welcomed in with open arms. His father even sees him from far off and ran to him. God is excited when we come to Him. He runs to us. The Creator of the Universe runs to meet us. God's Love does not want us to suffer. He wants us to be met with Grace when we turn to Him. If we are constantly in rebellion and in sin that is another story. He will use whatever it takes to get our attention. It is best to avoid this process!

Now when bad things start happening to us, we think that God hates us, but that is not true. Bad things happen to everyone on the Planet. When we are in sin, we don't expect God to bless us abundantly. We may get arrogant and think that God should or has to bless us, but He doesn't. He will never leave you or forsake you. He loves you and wants you to repent and turn to Him. Condemnation comes from the enemy. God will lovingly nudge you and convict you to repent, but He will not YELL AT YOU! He will warn you and plead with you, but He will not force you. He will use Preachers, strangers, and Christians to preach to you. He will use dreams, visions, and other ways to speak to you. There is a conviction at every turn when you are in sin. It is tough to ignore God when you are in sin. He will never stop! He loves you so much that He will not allow you to get comfortable in your sin. Jonah got comfortable in his sin, but He knew God could reach all the way out to the middle of the ocean to get him. But he thought he just needed a nap from obeying God! Wow. Don't take naps! God will reward those who diligently seek Him! Don't give up for in due season you will reap a harvest if you do not faint! AMEN!

So, you can fall into one or two traps with condemnation. You can sin and then get convicted but not want to face God, so you run from Him. Secondly, you can sin and then let the Devil beat you up until you repent. Either way, you allow condemnation to control you. The condemnation from the enemy is oppressive. You could sin and decide to run from God because you think He will not forgive you. You may feel that you are not ready for His forgiveness. You will avoid repenting and be condemned continually by the enemy. Condemnation tells you that you have disobeyed God, and you might as well just keep on sinning. The Devil convinces you to go deeper into sin. Once you do, then he condemns you for doing it. He just keeps you in the trap of condemnation by telling you that you are not good enough to return to God. A lie the enemy will say to you is, "You disobeyed God, and He is done with you now" or "You have gone too far away from God, and He will not take you back." The Devil has a whole bunch of lies. The Bible says that whatever you have done, God will forgive you if you ask.

The enemy is also happy if you sin and allow Him to beat you up after you have asked God to forgive you. We, as humans, operate on a reward system in this society. If you do good to me, then I will do good to you. If you offend me, then I will reward you with evil as well. When we sin, the enemy wants us to think that God is like this toward us. The way God has handled sin is from the beginning of time to the end of time. At the moment, Jesus was hanging on the cross, God collected all sin from the beginning of time till the end of time, and then He took all of it and placed it on Jesus. Jesus atoned for all sin at once. At one point, Jesus said, "My God My God, why have You forsaken Me." At this point is where He felt the sin of the World resting on Him. Sin is not acceptable to God, and God turned His Back in judgment of sin. Jesus felt that on the cross. This is how we can experience salvation at a future point from when Jesus died on the cross. Salvation is not an evolving process that needs to be added to by anyone.

So, unlike the Catholic Religion, we as Bible-Believing Christians do not believe in things that are not mentioned in the Bible. So, we do not believe in purgatory. If you are saved, and you have unconfessed sin, then you go to Heaven. Unconfessed sin doesn't mean that it isn't forgiven sin. Unconfessed sin feels like unforgiven sin because we feel the guilt and condemnation of that sin momentarily. We have to pray and give that guilt and condemnation to God continually, so we can feel God's Forgiveness and Love. That does not give us the right or license to go out and sin Romans 6:1-4 says,

"What shall we say then? Shall we continue in sin that grace may abound? Certainly not! How shall we who died to sin live any longer in it? Or do you not know that as many of us as were baptized into Christ Jesus were baptized into His death? Therefore, we were buried with Him through baptism into death, that just as Christ was raised from the dead by the glory of the Father, even so, we also should walk in newness of life."

We can continue in sin, but it just heaps up more guilt and condemnation, and the enemy takes up a room in our house and condemns and controls us. When the contract has nothing but torment day after day it will make you miserable and you will be exhausted. You are chained to the contract even though you do not understand all of the ramifications of what Condemnation does to you. I repeat this to help you understand the Devil has deceived you by every contract you have signed. We must return to God's Loving Arms to receive forgiveness and encouragement to continue walking with Him.

Now when we sin, the Devil wants us to get into a loop or pattern of sin. He wants us to sin, and then he wants to condemn us of sin. He wants this pattern to keep repeating, so we never feel worthy enough to repent. He also wants us to get used to sin and to ignore God. We tell ourselves that we will just stop doing whatever sin it is, and things will get better. The opposite happens. We continue sinning, and it always gets worse. Once you sin and care that you have sinned, then you beat yourself up over it. I do not know how many times I have sinned and allowed the enemy to talk to me afterward. He tells me, "Wow, you really did it this time, you don't care about the Lord at all and you are a hypocrite." Then because I know I have sinned; I feel bad immediately. I know that I did it, and I know that God is not pleased that I have sinned. I throw a giant pity party and allow the Devil to bring all of his demons. I sit back and allow spirits to beat me up to the point of depression. During this time, it can lead to more sin and further torture and guilt. I used to let this go for a week or more. I would sin and then just beat myself up. I had thrown such a terrible party that the enemy probably did not feel the need to be there because I was such a good party planner. I had agreed to and signed the Devil's Contract of Condemnation.

It got to the point that I knew I would have to take a minimum of a few days just to sit around and let the Devil beat me up. I would go into a depression and just isolate and watch T.V. or do something mind-numbing. I knew that my true passion of being used by the Lord would have to be put on the back burner while the Devil oppressed me with condemnation. We wind up, punishing ourselves and letting the Devil punish us also. There are religious spirits that accompany this condemnation as well. You punish yourself or let the enemy punish you because you aren't perfect. He retaliates with a lie like this, "After all you knew the Bible and knew it was sin," and "You know how not to sin, so you are worthless." If you beat yourself up over it, then He will shove your nose in it like a dog that pooped on the carpet. We have to repent from our sin and try not to sin again, right? No. We have to repent from the sin but get close to God in every way possible, so He can fill us with His Spirit so we can conquer sin. When we are tempted and have the Armor on then, we are ready to fight against sin. The Armor of God is supernatural, and we have to go to God to put it on (Ephesians 6).

If we are not in God's Armor, then the Devil knows it, and He comes running to tempt us because he knows he can get us to sin eventually. God will speak to you in a gentle, Loving Voice when talking with you. When you are tempted, He gives you a way out 1 Corinthians 10:12-13,

> *"Therefore, let him who thinks he stands take heed lest he fall. No temptation has overtaken you except such as is common to man, but God is faithful, who will not allow you to be tempted beyond what you are able, but with the temptation will also make the way of escape, that you may be able to bear it."*

You are never tempted beyond what you are able to bear. The way sin happens is so overwhelming that you usually don't have much time to prepare. There is a small window where you have a choice. You get tempted, and it is like there is a vast shadow that starts to rise on the wall of your soul. You see the shadow rising up, and you know that it is about to overtake you. At that moment, you have the choice to obey it or to run from it and pray. God will give you constant Love and warning as you are being tempted. God will not condemn you but will tell you He loves you and encourage you to get up and seek Him if you choose to sin. God is a loving God that will not yell at you or encourage you to quit. God knows why you fail and sin. It is because you are not walking close enough to Him to conquer sin. You are led away by Satan and worn down with temptation until you sin.

Reoccurring sin or committing to sin is a horrible thing to do. It is a commendable thing to be in a place that you do not have any sin that you are committing in your life. When I say commit, I mean not just doing once, it is a sin that you have allowed permission to take over at any time. You have given yourself to that sin. You may resist sometimes, but it is sporadic and the temptation to sin is more of an invitation to sin that you have already agreed to do. If you have reoccurring sin that you have committed to, then the Contract of Condemnation is in full force.

You have made up your mind that you want your sin over everything else. You have chosen to silence the Voice of God in any way It comes to you. You don't want to hear preaching about sin and refuse to repent. This brings condemnation upon you from the enemy. God will also deal harshly with those that are unwilling to repent. This is different from someone who is dabbling in sin and will repent quickly. When you choose sin over God, you make that thing your idol, and it will ruin your life if you continuously choose it over God. The Devil will lie to you and tell you that you should not pray and go to God because you feel like a hypocrite for not doing the right thing. God showed me that if we do not go to Him and pray after sinning that this is what makes us a hypocrite. Running from God because we think we should have done better is what is hypocritical not doing the sin itself. We cannot serve God without following Him and using the Power of the Holy Spirit and prayer to overcome sin. If we run from Him and try to do a better job next time then we are being a hypocrite. We need to run straight back to God and repent from sinning right away despite how we feel or what condemning lies the Devil is telling us.

We must repent of the sin that is in our life, so we are not condemned by the Devil. It is an oppressing place to have the Devil beating you up and controlling you with condemnation. Romans 8:1 says, "*There is therefore now no condemnation to those who are in Christ Jesus, who do not walk according to the flesh, but according to the Spirit.*" You can experience a life free from condemnation if you are in Christ Jesus. If you walk a life pleasing to God in the Spirit (not trying to be perfect in the efforts of the flesh), then you will not be condemned Galatians 5:18 says, "But if you are led by the Spirit, you are not under the law." The Law can't condemn you, and neither can Satan if you are walking in the Spirit. If you are yielding your life to God, then there are no laws that have been broken. The Devil does not have a right to condemn you Galatians 5:22-25 says,

"But the fruit of the Spirit is love, joy, peace, longsuffering, kindness, goodness, ,faithfulness, gentleness, self-control. Against such, there is no law. And those who are Christ's have crucified the flesh with its passions and desires. If we live in the Spirit, let us also walk in the Spirit"

It is time for us to live a life that is pleasing to God, so we will not be condemned. If you have sin in your life that you need to repent for, then the Holy Spirit is showing you this daily. Now is the time to confess this sin and get the Devil out of your life. You can tell where the Devil is hiding in your life because he will show up in your thoughts, speech, and actions. He has the right to condemn you because you have broken the Law of God. He will chase after you until you surrender to his voice of condemnation. It is oppressive and demonic. Jesus said He comes to set the captives free. If you surrender to Jesus, He will evict the Devil out of your life and set you free. No matter what you have done the Lord will forgive you Psalm 103:2-4,

"Bless the Lord, O my soul, and forget not all His benefits: Who forgives all your sins, who heals all your diseases, who redeems your life from destruction, who crowns you with loving-kindness and tender mercies."

The Lord is willing to forgive you for any sins that you have committed. The Bible says all sins in verse 3, and this means all. Today is the day to get free from your past and allow the Blood of Jesus to wash you clean of all past sins and hurts. Joshua 24:15 says,

"And if it seems evil to you to serve the Lord, choose for yourselves this day whom you will serve, whether the gods which your fathers served that were on the other side of the river or the gods of the Amorites, in whose land you dwell. But as for me and my house, we will serve the Lord."

Jesus told the Parable of the Prodigal Son (Luke 15:11-32). This Parable is about a son that did not want to live at home any longer. He asked for his inheritance from the father, and he left. He spent all of his money, and before long, he was living with the pigs. He realized that he could come home and not have to live like a homeless person or farm animal. When he went home, finally, he received a warm welcome from the father who came running to meet him. God wants you to come home and stop living a life of emptiness, regret, and condemnation. Surrendering to the Lord is rewarding and is the ultimate freedom anyone can ever experience.

Your past cannot tower over you anymore if you bring it to God. He will heal you from condemnation. The past cannot be changed it is done. We cannot undo our past mistakes. The eggs have been broken and the omelet has been made. Psalm 103:2-4 says, *"Praise the Lord, my soul, and forget not all his benefits who forgives all your sins and heals all your diseases, who redeems your life from the pit and crowns you with love and compassion."* God will forgive you of all of your sins, not just the ones you think are really bad. Open up to God and tell Him your secrets and let go of your shame. The past is God's Territory now and only He can deal with it. We have all tried and it has driven us insane.

The Devil will torment you continuously until you release the past to God. Once you have given it to God then the Devil will try to bring it back up again but we can quote Scripture to him to put him in his place. Let God do His Job and give you a clean slate. He has determined this is the way it should be. Relax in the Plan of God. Romans 8:38-39 says,

"For I am persuaded that neither death nor life, nor angels nor principalities nor powers, nor things present nor things to come, nor height nor depth, nor any other created thing, shall be able to separate us from the love of God which is in Christ Jesus our Lord."

The Devil will try to separate us from God by deceiving and condemning us. We must fight the enemy and get back in the Presence of God. God will never leave us or forsake us. When we cannot feel God in our lives it does not mean that He has left us or stopped loving us. We just need to go and get in God's Presence and we will be able to feel His Loving Embrace.

Let's choose to serve the Lord and reject sin and Satan out of our lives. Repeat this prayer out loud and mean it with all of your heart with all sincerity. "Heavenly Father, I accept Your Love for my life. I accept that You Love me. I have sinned against You, and I need Your Forgiveness. Please forgive me for all of my sins. I cannot walk this Christian walk without You. I need to be close to You. Please wash me clean and give me a new start. I need Your Help to fight the enemy. Lord, empower me to serve You. I renounce Satan in my life. I renounce all lies of condemnation I believed. Nothing can separate me from the Love of God in Christ Jesus. I Break the Contract of Condemnation in Jesus Name. I accept your Love. Fill me with Your Spirit and Peace. Help me to hear Your Loving Voice. Help me to know You. I surrender to You today and make You Lord of my Life. In Jesus Name, I pray. Amen."

Saints let's rejoice that the Voice of the Lord is a Loving Voice. He is excited to meet us every time we pray. Let's not allow anything keep us from prayer. When we sin, let's run to pray and receive God's Mercy and not allow the enemy to get us to sin again or beat us up with condemnation! You have successfully authorized the Lord to eject Satan out of another room in your temple! Let's continue on allowing the Lord to set us free! Amen!

CHAPTER 10

The Contract of Worldliness

"Adulterers and adulteresses! Do you not know that friendship with the world is enmity with God? Whoever therefore wants to be a friend of the world makes himself an enemy of God." James 4:4

There are areas of compromise in our lives that keep us from truly getting close to the Lord. In the Outer Court of the Old Testament's Tabernacle, we see that the High Priest is just continually doing purification rituals and making sacrifices. The High Priest never gets to fulfill his purpose in a New Testament role. If the minister stays in the Outer Courts just doing rituals, then it is a colossal waste of purpose and service to the Lord. Today many people are still in the Outer Court, and they are just continually confessing their sins, saying prayers to God, and not doing Ministry but having a whole lot of opinions. This leads to worldliness and no real personal, intimate relationship with God. Worldliness is falling into the ways of the World and disregarding the ways of Christ.

A simple definition of worldliness is to relax or not take the Word of God seriously to obey it. Worldliness is giving into sin and allowing it to control you. This mindset says it ok to not go to Church, act like non-believers, blend in with the crowd, not follow Christ or let your light shine to the World. A worldly Christian would be someone who says they believe in God but they are not committed to Christ. They would not read their Bible, go to Church, or witness to others. They will be comfortable in their sin and not want to repent. Their speech will be corrupted with the things of this World. They would even debate why they should follow the Word of God with complete obedience. Worldly Christians have placed their self and their own interests above the Word of God.

If you wake up and do your thing all day long and pray for forgiveness at the end of the day, you will not be getting anywhere with God. You live the dangerous lie of sinning, being used by the enemy, and then thinking you are righteous at the end of the day by a quick prayer. It is a deception of the enemy and not a genuine walk with God. Micah 6:8 says, "_He has shown you, O man, what is good; And what does the Lord require of you But to do justly, To love mercy, And to walk humbly with your God?_" This requires humility to walk regularly with God in obedience, not just saying a quick prayer at night and falling asleep halfway through. The Bible says that being a friend with the World is sinful in James 4:4-5,

> _"Adulterers and adulteresses! Do you not know that friendship with the world is enmity with God? Whoever therefore wants to be a friend of the world makes himself an enemy of God. Or do you think that the Scripture says in vain, The Spirit who dwells in us yearns jealously?"_

Worldliness is considered demonic and makes you an Enemy of God. God is a Jealous God (Exodus 20:5), and He wants us to serve Him and not this World. He longs for us jealously with a healthy love and compassion. We have to realize that if we are worldly, then we are serving the enemy. Without faith, it is impossible to please God. We can't live a life that is dedicated to this World and think we are serving God. We should have a counter-culture mindset. This culture leads us to believe naturally and abandon the faith and supernatural things. To be a cheerleader for the culture is sinful. This culture supports evil and calls evil good. It says support same-sex lifestyles and punishes those who preach against it. It says it is ok to live with someone before marriage, and it doesn't even matter his or her sexual orientation.

This culture supports Christians not going to Church. "God will forgive me for not going," or "I hate Church with all of these hypocritical Christians." Your opinion is wrong if it does not line up with the Word of God. God instituted the Church and gave Gifts and Offices for the Church and told us to not forsake the gathering together for Church in Hebrews 10:25, "_Not forsaking the assembling of ourselves together, as is the manner of some, but exhorting one another, and so much the more as you see the Day approaching._" It doesn't matter what reason you have for justifying what you believe. Paul says that we are not to be like some people (Worldly people) that don't go to Church, but we are to assemble with other Believers for God's Will and Purposes. You might not want to go to Church because your life is not right with God. This is not an excuse to disobey the Word of God. If you understand this message but do not want to comply, then you are rebellious, your pride keeps you from serving the Lord, and the Devil is happy about it. You are being worldly and helping the enemy by being an Enemy of God. However, you say oh no, I'm not an enemy of God. I love God. Well, do you obey His Word? If you are not going to Church, then you are in disobedience.

Why am I emphasizing this? The Great Commission is never going to happen if Christians don't participate in it. The Devil tells Christians not to go to Church because you can hear a sermon at home. This is correct. The Devil tells you that you don't have to go to Church to be a Christian. This is technically correct. The Devil tells you to have a day of rest and that you need to get your sleep. This is correct. The Devil will give you a thousand reasons not to go to Church, but these are all half-truths. They all have an aspect of truth to it, so we just eat it up like Eve and then are punished. You are supposed to go to Church to be encouraged and to help people. It is not only about you! Ouch. I know that hurt, but it is true. When God anoints you, it is always for someone else. What? Yes. The Anointing comes and rests on one person so the other person can receive it and be blessed by it. We are blessed in the process. It is incredible and such an honor to be unworthy (Qualified by our own merits), but used by God. His Grace is truly Amazing!

God is not going to pour out His Anointing into the Dead Sea or someone with no outlet. The Dead Sea in Jerusalem has no outlet. It is a dead-end street. We are dead and empty if we are not letting God pour His Anointing on us so we can let it constantly flow like a river to others. God wants you to move, and then you will see the Gifts of the Spirit active in your life. He wants you to have a reason to use your faith. In America it seems we only have faith that the fridge stays cold, or the internet and electricity remain on during a storm. We are so comfortable in America that we are losing our purpose, and it is causing the Church to seem weak. Before the internet was used for everything, we had to go out and meet people and be interactive, and this is how God wants it today. Get up off the couch and throw your excuses in the trash. You can binge-watch those shows later. The days are short, and people need your help. You may think that you have nothing to offer, but you are wrong, and the Devil has been lying to you.

God has uniquely planted in all of us a unique set of skills and Gifts. Use your skills and help someone. We are all the Body of Christ, and we need each other. Help guide people to the Truth. Use this book as a weapon against the enemy. Help people get free from the Contracts they have signed with Satan. Have Bible studies with family and friends using this book and praying at the end of every chapter. Get the WORD OUT! If you are busy doing good things, then you are just boxing the air as Paul says in 1 Corinthians 9:26, "*So I do not run like someone who doesn't run toward the finish line. I do not fight like a boxer who hits nothing but air.*" We must focus on fulfilling our purpose and goals in life.

If you don't connect to other people who need your help, you will not get the help you need either because God uses other people to help us all the time. The Bible says that we have Offices in the Church that need to be fulfilled Ephesians 4:11-12, "*And He Himself gave some to be apostles, some prophets, some evangelists, and some pastors and teachers, for the equipping of the saints for the work of ministry, for the edifying of the body of Christ.*" God designed this so you can be equipped for the work of Ministry and edified. The Devil does not want that to happen, and if you serve the enemy, you will stay out of the Church. However, if you're going to serve God, you will go to Church, which is His Will. I have had plenty of people tell me they are ok not going to Church. They have all signed a Contract of Worldliness with the Devil. This Contract prevents them from being blessed by God and getting set free from demonic strongholds. Instead, this Contract forces you to serve the Devil by being worldly. There is no solution for this except to repent.

We have to repent from our excuses and preferences and serve God. You have a purpose in the Church and God really wants you to help others Ephesians 4:16, "*From whom the whole body, joined and knit together by what every joint supplies, according to the effective working by which every part does its share, causes growth of the body for the edifying of itself in love.*" Every part does its share, and that causes growth for the Body of Christ. If you love God, then you will help His Body function correctly. You are a part of the Body, and you cannot say to the Hand I don't need you or to the Foot, I don't need you. We must stop doing good things and do God things. We must stop with our great commission and help fulfill the Great Commission. We will be held accountable for disobeying the Word of God.

The Contract of Worldliness can be tough to break. This Contract allows us to be comfortable. Today this World is full of comforts. This whole society is all about convenience. We don't want to have to leave our house if we don't need to. This threatens our free time and our lifestyle. If we are worldly, then we don't have to be inconvenienced. However, we are considered an Enemy of God if we are friends with the World. I don't know about you, but God doesn't treat His Enemies very well from what we learned in the last chapter. We all must count the cost and decide to break every area of the Contract.

There is not one Contract that is worth being an Enemy of God, is there? When you count the cost, you have to make sure to make up your mind. Jesus said in Luke 9:62, "*But Jesus said to him, "No one, having put his hand to the plow, and looking back, is fit for the kingdom of God.*" The Kingdom of God is a thing that is reserved for the people who are dedicated to the Lord and that have faith. The Kingdom of God is the Power of God coming upon those walking in faith. Jesus said that when you heal someone, tell them the Kingdom of God has come upon them. You can't be double minded as a Christian. All Christians are supposed to be in Ministry at their Church and marketplace. We are witnesses everywhere we go.

If you want to serve God, you cannot go 90 percent of the way and quit. This is a serious call from the Lord, and you have to make sure you are ready to answer it. I know that you are, but you cannot cling to the World. You must let go. Your identity is hidden in Christ and not in this World. Colossians 3:1-3 says,

"If then you have been raised with Christ, seek the things that are above, where Christ is, seated at the right hand of God. Set your minds on things that are above, not on things that are on earth. For you have died, and your life is hidden with Christ in God."

Sometimes, it is scary to take a leap of faith, get out of the boat, and walk on water. The others I'm sure criticized Peter for getting out of the boat and falling in the water. However, they were envious of him because they didn't have the guts to take that step of faith. It is the same for the worldly people. When you get out of the boat, then the worldly people will be motivated to serve God. Faith is inspiring, and you will give others the hope they need to get motivated to serve God. I have seen it happen in my life repeatedly.

Jesus describes the Word of God in a parable as Seed. If you have good tilled fertile ground, then the Word of God can grow easily. If you have bad soil, then the Seed will not be able to grow correctly. There are conditions that Jesus gives for the growth of that Seed. Most of these conditions are harmful to the seed as you can see in Matthew 13:3-9,

"Then He spoke many things to them in parables, saying: "Behold, a sower went out to sow. And as he sowed, some seed fell by the wayside; and the birds came and devoured them. Some fell on stony places, where they did not have much earth; and they immediately sprang up because they had no depth of earth. But when the sun was up, they were scorched, and because they had no root they withered away. And some fell among thorns, and the thorns sprang up and choked them. But others fell on good ground and yielded a crop: some a hundredfold, some sixty, some thirty. He who has ears to hear, let him hear!"

You are the one in whom the seed can be planted. If your heart is not ready to allow the seed in to grow, then you will reject it. You can even blame God if you want, but it's not His fault. We have to break the Devil's Contract and repent from our sin. We must turn to God in order to receive the Word of God on good ground (vs. 8). Hear what the Spirit of the Lord is saying through the Word. A mustard seed can fall into good soil and grow into a massive tree or be rejected by the soil. Repent and have faith in the Word of God.

The Lord loves to Bless His People when they are obedient to Him. I want you to understand how the Lord works with blessing His People. God has a plan for us to obey Him and be blessed. The Blessings of the Lord, as seen with Job, protect us from the enemy. Now, these blessings are conditional. God will bless you if you obey Him. God's Blessings are conditional, but His Love is unconditional. You have to accept Jesus to be saved, but He has already unconditionally made the sacrifice. All you have to do is accept His Love. Nevertheless, if you want to be blessed by God, then there are many things He wants us to do. However, His Blessings are Amazing and worth it. I have never been one to go crazy over serving the Lord for future rewards or afterlife blessings. Many people will say, "I am going to have a big mansion in Heaven," or "God will bless me if I tithe." All of these things are true, but our motivation should be to serve God out of gratefulness.

Being able to help other people is a blessing in itself. It makes you feel fantastic to help someone who needs and wants help. Did you know that some people don't want the Lord to help them? It's crazy, but I have met several people like this. They want to do it the hard way. God resists the proud but gives Grace to the humble 1 Peter 5:5-6,

"Likewise, you younger people, submit yourselves to your elders. Yes, all of you be submissive to one another, and be clothed with humility, for "God resists the proud, but gives grace to the humble." Therefore, humble yourselves under the mighty hand of God, that He may exalt you in due time."

Speaking of being humble, we must daily submit to the Lord in spending time with Him. God wants us to have humility that causes us to spend time with Him to be more like Him.

We have to repent from our callused heart toward sin to end worldliness. The Bible says we are to renew our minds daily. How are we doing this by watching television, apps on our phone, working a lot, spending time with other people, or doing activities? No. This is to be done by reading the Word of God Romans 12:1-2 says,

"I beseech you therefore, brethren, by the mercies of God, that you present your bodies a living sacrifice, holy, acceptable to God, which is your reasonable service. And do not be conformed to this world, but be transformed by the renewing of your mind, that you may prove what is that good and acceptable and perfect will of God."

Reading the Word of God gets your eyes involved, and you can take the time to study Scripture or write it down. You can listen to sermons all day long if you want, or the digital Bible. You can leave it going all day long, and the Lord will speak to you. You will be renewing your mind. As far as the best way to renew your mind, I would suggest reading the Word of God. This is best because you can control where the Lord wants to take you through the Scriptures, and it is a journey. You can underline them and write notes all in your Bible, and it is incredible.

We are going to make sure all of the rooms in your house are empty. This is critical to devote yourself to the Lord fully. You do not want to give an open door to Satan. The Bible says that if we give the Devil a foothold, then he will destroy our lives. This foothold will lead to greater sins and division between you and God's people. I want you to ask the Lord what you need to repent about today. This is a serious question because you are trying to identify all of the areas the Devil is active in your life. Make a list. The first thing you can put on the list is pride. I don't care who you are. If you say you have no pride, then you are prideful. The goal of this is, to be honest, and have humility. God resists the proud but gives Grace and Favor to the humble. You have to find the place and time or reason you signed the Contract to whatever sin you cannot conquer. We have more than one area of sin in our lives.

We have to put God first daily and allow Him to move in our lives through our obedience to Him. Do an honest inventory of your idols and sins. We want the Lord to clean out our lives from evil like it says in Psalm 51:10, *"Create in me a clean heart, O God, and renew a steadfast spirit within me."* The Lord will guide you in repentance. The voice of the enemy will order you to sin, and it seems like you have no choice. These areas of your life are not submitted to God, and they need to come under the Authority of Jesus Christ. Prepare a list of these things and anything else the Holy Spirit shows you, and let's pray. I have made an outline for you at the end of the book. Complete the outline now and get ready to pray over it.

Repeat this prayer out loud, and let's pray! "Heavenly Father, I come to You today in humility. I need Your Help, Lord. I cannot seem to walk in Your Ways because of my sin. Please forgive me Lord, for my sins. I am sorry, and I don't want to do these sins anymore because they are evil. I want more of You. I renounce Satan in my life. I confess all of these sins to You Lord. Holy Spirit, I need You to deliver me. I release my will for my life. I repent of my rebellion to your Word. I repent for every place I have taken You off the throne in my life. God cleanse me by Your Blood. Please break all of these strongholds off my life and allow me to have freedom. You said where the Spirit of the Lord is; there is freedom. Lord, free me from these chains. I Break the Contract of Worldliness in Jesus Name. I renounce you Satan, you are not my master anymore and you do not control me. I rebuke you in Jesus Name. I renounce all of your lies. Help me Lord Jesus to daily walk with you and to put you first. Help me to read Your Word and understand It. Help me apply It to my walk and obey You instead of doing what my flesh wants to do. Lord, I love You. In Jesus Name, I pray. Amen." Let's study about the Power of God in chapter 11.

CHAPTER 11

The Unmatched Power of God

"Behold, I am the Lord, the God of all flesh. Is there anything too hard for Me?" Jeremiah 32:27

Let's begin with a quick mental challenge. Think quickly and answer these questions with the direct opposite of the example given. Here is a sample question. What is the opposite of poor? The answer is rich. The opposite of day is? The opposite of big is? The opposite of left is? The opposite of God is? Well, if you answered the Devil, then this is a common answer. Since God created Satan, then God has no equal. No one created Him. God is the creator of all things, including the Devil. The Devil was an Angel in Heaven that God gave the job of leading worship. God is Omnipresent, Omnipotent, and Omniscient. God is the only being that is Omnipresent, which means He can be everywhere at once. God is Omnipotent, which means He is All-Powerful. This means that He is unmatched in His Power. He has given us His Power over the enemy. Exciting to think about, isn't it? God is also Omniscient, which means He is All-Knowing. This is the reason that all prophecies in the Bible are 100 percent accurate, and all of them will come to pass. This is an easy way to prove that the Bible is actually the Word of God.

Demonic spirits and the power of the enemy are very evident in the Bible. They torment people and possess them. We see examples in the Old and New Testament. The Old Testament has a story of Satan in Job. He is standing in front of God, trying to talk to Him about Job. Satan is talking about how God has blessed Job, and there was no way for him to reach Job. God's Blessing was so Powerful that even Satan himself could not penetrate It Job 1:9-12 says,

"So, Satan answered the Lord and said, "Does Job fear God for nothing? Have You not made a hedge around him, around his household, and around all that he has on every side? You have blessed the work of his hands, and his possessions have increased in the land. But now, stretch out Your hand and touch all that he has, and he will surely curse You to Your face!" And the Lord said to Satan, "Behold, all that he has is in your power; only do not lay a hand on his person. "Therefore, Satan went out from the presence of the Lord."

There is a lot to learn from this passage about Satan and his power. He is limited to what God will allow him to do to His People. Satan spoke of the Blessing of God being so POWERFUL that he could not breach it. He talked about the Blessing of God on the hands of Job and the blessings of his possessions. The Power of God was so strong on Job's life that the enemy needed permission. Oh, and the enemy had to obey God! God said not to touch his life, and Satan could not.

His servants of darkness or witches have power but do not match with the Power of God. Let us look at the book of Exodus to see this in Exodus 7:8-12,

"Then the Lord spoke to Moses and Aaron, saying, "When Pharaoh speaks to you, saying, 'Show a miracle for yourselves,' then you shall say to Aaron, 'Take your rod and cast it before Pharaoh and let it become a serpent.' So, Moses and Aaron went into Pharaoh, and they did so, just as the Lord commanded. And Aaron cast down his rod before Pharaoh and before his servants, and it became a serpent. But Pharaoh also called the wise men and the sorcerers; so, the magicians of Egypt, they also did in like manner with their enchantments. For every man threw down his rod, and they became serpents. But Aaron's rod swallowed up their rods."

The sorcerers had power from the Devil but could not even hold a candle to the Power of God's Anointed Object. Therefore, we see that the Devil is limited, and his sorcerers are second-rate dime store magicians compared to an Object anointed by God. The Anointing or Power of God is stronger than dark magic. Satan's Kingdom has power and that draws some people to him. We must be prepared to show the Power of God so we can be a witness to these people and show God to be the All-Powerful Merciful King of the Universe!

Let us move on and try to find something that can at least match the Power of God. I do not think that we will find anything in the entire Bible, hence the name of this chapter, but let us keep looking. Therefore, we will journey to the story of the Prophet Elijah. This is an extraordinary story, and I love it so much. Wow. Elijah was so bold and knew the Power of God that he taunted the enemy with it. Amazing. Elijah used his faith, 1 Kings 18:25-29 says,

"Now Elijah said to the prophets of Baal, "Choose one bull for yourselves and prepare it first, for you are many; and call on the name of your god but put no fire under it." So, they took the bull which was given them, and they prepared it and called on the name of Baal from morning even till noon, saying, "O Baal, hear us!" But there was no voice; no one answered. Then they leaped about the altar which they had made. And so it was, at noon, that Elijah mocked them and said, "Cry aloud, for he is a god; either he is meditating, or he is busy, or he is on a journey, or perhaps he is sleeping and must be awakened." So, they cried aloud, and cut themselves, as was their custom, with knives and lances, until the blood gushed out on them. And when midday was past, they prophesied until the time of the offering of the evening sacrifice. But there was no voice; no one answered, no one paid attention."

Maybe this is where the saying came from that your request has fallen on deaf ears? Sorry, I am a little drunk in the Spirit. It's amusing once you learn that Satan's power DOES NOT EVEN COME CLOSE to the UNMATCHED POWER OF GOD. Satan has people running scared because he has a loud bark. Let's look at the result here of 6 hours of hollering and screaming until their voices gave out. Their god Satan and the idols they served could not do anything for them. Imagine that! Serving idols your whole life, and then when it is time for them to show up, nothing happens. Good thing no one paid money to see Baal perform in this circus because he was a no show!

Elijah mocked them, and I am laughing out loud. He said, "Cry aloud, for he is a god; either he is meditating, or he is busy, or he is on a journey, or perhaps he is sleeping and must be awakened." He said, what? Wow. Maybe he is meditating, or he is busy? Maybe he is on a walkabout and can't be reached or has no cell signal? Elijah knew the Power of God and most importantly had a personal relationship with Him. The Bible says that the people who know their

God shall be strong and carry out great exploits (Daniel 11:32). We are to be fearless when it comes to being a witness for God.

Now it is the Prophet of the Lord's turn to shine. Wow, after all that trash talk, you had better be ready to put up or shut up. Well, he was ready 1 Kings 18:32-35 says,

"Then, with the stones he built an altar in the name of the Lord; and he made a trench around the altar large enough to hold two seahs of seed. And he put the wood in order, cut the bull in pieces, and laid it on the wood, and said, "Fill four water pots with water, and pour it on the burnt sacrifice and on the wood." Then he said, "Do it a second time," and they did it a second time; and he said, "Do it a third time," and they did it a third time. So, the water ran all around the altar, and he also filled the trench with water."

There was enough water on the altar and the offering to make sure all doubt would be erased for a possible magic trick. 1 Kings 18:38-39 says,

"Then the fire of the Lord fell and consumed the burnt sacrifice, and the wood and the stones and the dust, and it licked up the water that was in the trench. Now when all the people saw it, they fell on their faces; and they said, "The Lord, He is God! The Lord, He is God!"

Now the Lord made sure to back up His Prophet. God once again showed His Power. Not only did He make fire fall from Heaven, but also, He completely stopped up the enemy's magic and ability to burn up the offering on the altar. Therefore, we have Satan having to ask permission, the sorcerer's magic was gobbled up, and the false prophets were shut down. Now let us move on to the New Testament.

Jesus came to the Earth and had an encounter with Satan. He shut Satan down just by using the Word of God (Luke 4:1-13). Jesus had no problems with demons either Mark 5:11-13,

"Now a large herd of swine was feeding there near the mountains. So, all the demons begged Him, saying, "Send us to the swine, that we may enter them." And at once Jesus gave them permission. Then the unclean spirits went out and

entered the swine (there were about two thousand), and the herd ran violently down the steep place into the sea and drowned in the sea."

Once again, they begged Jesus for permission. Jesus didn't yell or scream. He just spoke. He has Authority. It's simple. They begged and pleaded. Jesus showed His Power over the works of the enemy Matthew 4:23-24,

"And Jesus went about all Galilee, teaching in their synagogues, preaching the gospel of the kingdom, and healing all kinds of sickness and all kinds of disease among the people. Then His fame went throughout all Syria, and they brought to Him all sick people who were afflicted with various diseases and torments, and those who were demon-possessed, epileptics, and paralytics; and He healed them."

He had no problems healing the sick or casting out demons. When it came to the supernatural power of the enemy, Jesus could not be harmed or intimidated. Jesus did willingly lay down His Life for sin, but it was His Choice. Jesus also appeared to over 500 people for 40 days before He went to the Father 1 Corinthians 15:3-8 says,

"For I delivered to you first of all that which I also received: that Christ died for our sins according to the Scriptures, and that He was buried, and that He rose again the third day according to the Scriptures, and that He was seen by Cephas, then by the twelve. After that, He was seen by over five hundred brethren at once, of whom the greater part remain to the present, but some have fallen asleep. After that, He was seen by James, then by all the apostles. Then last of all, He was seen by me also, as by one born out of due time."

So, Jesus resurrected and showed His Power over death and the grave. He walked around town and continued to show His Power.

Jesus went to the Father and He atoned for our sin. He did it by shedding His Blood 7 times on Earth as the High Priest. God released the Holy Spirit to fill the temple of believers. The Holy Spirit caused men to be born again. This empowerment allowed all Believers to become the Church. The Bible says that we are the Temple of God. The Holy Spirit fills us when we are born again, and now we are a temple for the Holy Spirit. We become a Church or Temple. Our bodies house the Holy Spirit of God. This includes the Power of God. So now, the Church or individual Believer has the same Power that Jesus had, which is the Holy Spirit. Jesus had the Holy Spirit's Power without measure. We are limited by our own free will and faith in this area. However, the source of Power is still the same. It is the Holy Spirit that came on Jesus after His Baptism and the same Holy Spirit fell at Pentecost in Acts 2:1-4,

"When the day of Pentecost came, they were all together in one place. Suddenly a sound like the blowing of a violent wind came from Heaven and filled the whole house where they were sitting. They saw what seemed to be tongues of fire that separated and came to rest on each of them. All of them were filled with the Holy Spirit and began to speak in other tongues as the Spirit enabled them."

Once these believers received the Promise that Jesus told them about as they waited in the upper room then they had power Acts 1:8 says, "*But you shall receive power when the Holy Spirit has come upon you, and you shall be witnesses to Me in Jerusalem, and in all Judea and Samaria, and to the end of the earth.*" Jesus gave His Believers the Holy Spirit. This is what happens to all Christians at the New Birth when they believe in Jesus and are born again. In Acts, we see several times that the Apostles healed people and cast out demons by the Power of God. Jesus gave them Power over the enemy and empowered them to fulfill the Great Commission and make disciples. We are commanded to believe God for miracles and cast out demons Mark 16:15-18,

"And He said to them, "Go into all the world and preach the gospel to every creature. He who believes and is baptized will be saved, but he who does not believe will be condemned. And these signs will follow those who believe: In My name, they will cast out demons; they will speak with new tongues: they will take up serpents; and if they drink anything deadly, it will by no means hurt them; they will lay hands on the sick, and they will recover."

All of these things are part of the Great Commission, and we are commissioned with the Power to go and preach to the whole World the saving Gospel of Jesus Christ. The enemy's administration has not ceased to exist and is very active. The Power of God is still active through the Holy Spirit in the temples of Believers. God uses Angels and the prayers of Christians to show His

Power as well. Christians are to go face to face and toe to toe with the enemy in this Dark Age. The Holy Spirit empowers Believers with Gifts and Anointing to handle the satanic magic, curses, and demons that try to attack believers.

Do not try to fight demonic forces without knowing your authority in Christ. I am not trying to scare you or to intimidate you. We see that the Power of God is too mighty for satanic forces. If you do not have or believe in the Power of God within you, you will not be successful. Acts 19 has a powerful story about a similar situation. Acts 19:13-16,

"Then some of the itinerant Jewish exorcists took it upon themselves to call the name of the Lord Jesus over those who had evil spirits, saying, "We exorcise you by the Jesus whom Paul preaches." Also, there were seven sons of Sceva, a Jewish chief priest, who did so. And the evil Spirit answered and said, "Jesus I know, and Paul I know; but who are you?" Then the man in whom the evil Spirit was leaped on them, overpowered them and prevailed against them so that they fled out of that house naked and wounded."

In verse 14, it says, "We exorcise you by the Jesus whom Paul preaches." This is an indirect relationship. This type of authority does not work. They did not have a personal relationship with Jesus. They were not confident that this would work because they didn't have the Power within them or the Authority to do it. The demon said, "Jesus, I know, and Paul, I know; but who are you?"

This was what you would call a rhetorical question. The demons knew the answer. Everyone involved knew the answer. They were nobody, and they were treated like nobody! It says the evil spirits beat them up, and they barely made it out of there, running naked and wounded. The Devil will make a fool out of you if you try to fight him without Christ's Power. If you are a Spirit-Filled Christian, then you have the Holy Spirit, and you will be ok. God has your back, and the forces of darkness will not overtake you! You will overtake them by the Power of God, and they will have to flee! Always make sure to listen to God on the correct timing to cast out demons and how to handle each situation because they are all different. Some demons only come out by fasting and prayer (Matthew17:21).

The Power of God is real, and it has been proved repeatedly in the Old Testament by snakes being eaten up and offerings being burnt up. God is not afraid to show His Power, and every time He does it is a chance to minister and show His Power so others will repent Acts 19:17-20,

> *"This became known both to all Jews and Greeks dwelling in Ephesus, and fear fell on them all, and the name of the Lord Jesus was magnified. And many who had believed came confessing and telling their deeds. Also, many of those who had practiced magic brought their books together and burned them in the sight of all. And they counted up the value of them, and it totaled fifty thousand pieces of silver. So, the word of the Lord grew mightily and prevailed."*

People who are serving the enemy do it for many different reasons. When the Power of God is manifested, it exposes the weakness of the Devil and his kingdom. Many people will repent as these people did. They burned all of their books and repented.

There are many different Religions and things the enemy uses to cause you to serve him. False Religions, cults, witchcraft, Ouija boards, spells, chants, palm readers, and good luck charms are all evil devices the enemy uses to deceive people. We must not participate in any of these demonic activities or give power to any trinkets or items. As the Lord used handkerchiefs with Paul, the same type of items can be cursed with demonic energy. It is time to repent if you have participated in any kind of demonic activity. You must rid your house of any sinister or evil items you have collected or that was given to you. Pray and take a tour around your home. The Holy Spirit will show you if you have any items that He disapproves of you having. Don't question God or the value of the thing you are throwing away. They burned their witchcraft books, and the total money value was 50 thousand pieces of silver. Obey God and get rid of it. You can throw it away outside of your house.

Things you should throw away would include literature for other Religions and scriptures from other Religions like Mormonism, demonic books, and symbols or trinkets. Horror movies or books that have satanic stories in them should be trashed. Things involving the occult or satanic things should be thrown away. These items create strongholds in the house and hinder the Spirit of God. Anything else the Holy Spirit shows you that could lead you to sin or that is sinful should also be thrown away. Items that rob you of peace or that you question should just be thrown away. You should have total peace when you walk around your home. Jesus is the Prince of Peace. When you are done, throw all of the stuff in the trashcan outside of your home. Ask God to forgive you for having these items in your home and invite the Holy Spirit to come into your house and rest there, bringing Peace.

Let's pray against the participation of any demonic activity or involvement you have done in your life. If you are currently involved in anything the Lord would not approve of, then it is time to confess these things and repent. Your allegiance lies with Jesus and not anyone or anything else. If you have participated in evil like witchcraft, vengeful demonic prayers, or anything mentioned in this chapter then you have invited a demonic stronghold into your life. You agreed to a Contract allowing demonic possession or oppression to plague you. You must repent and renounce any ties with satanic activity. It doesn't matter if you only participated, or you were a leader in the Church of Satan. This is serious, and you have to renounce Satan. Let's pray and allow God's Unmatched Power to break any ties with Satan that you have made.

Pray this prayer with faith and all of your heart. "Heavenly Father, I confess my sins to You today. If I have participated in anything demonic or satanic, please forgive me. I renounce my allegiance to any satanic activity or items. I renounce witchcraft and rebellion. Lord, I plead the Power of the Blood of Jesus to cleanse me. I believe in the POWER OF GOD, and I accept Your Love and Power in my life. Please cleanse me from all evil that I have committed. I am sorry for using that power, and I will not do it again. Help me to serve you. I Break the Contract of Witchcraft I have signed with the Devil. I renounce you Satan and command you to leave my life in Jesus Name. I will not follow you any longer. Shut up and leave! God You are the Almighty, and no one is more powerful than You are. Cleanse me, Lord, and allow Your Love to flow through me. Help me to be a witness to others. I make you Lord of my life. I am your servant, and you are my Master! In Jesus Name, I pray. Amen."

Now that we have repented from the works of darkness and have embraced God's real Power, then we are ready to use this Power against the enemy. God wants us to walk humbly with Him. The Christian life has obstacles, but nothing is too hard for God! You have cleaned out another room for God to dwell. You are becoming full of the Holy Spirit! Let's move on to learn more about walking with the Lord! I am proud of you for taking these steps of faith!

CHAPTER 12

The Abundant Life

"The thief does not come except to steal, and to kill, and to destroy. I have come that they may have life and that they may have it more abundantly." John 10:10

Jesus tells us that He came to give us life that is Abundant and Overflowing. Jesus wants us to have a life that is overflowing with the Spirit. Maybe you thought all Christians are supposed to just to go around broke, mad, and sick. Nope! Jesus told us the enemy's plan is to kill us, steal from us, and destroy us. Jesus wants to bless us and set us free. Now all of the Fruits of the Spirit are supernatural. Galatians 5:22-23 says, *"But the fruit of the Spirit is love, joy, peace, longsuffering, kindness, goodness, faithfulness, gentleness, self-control. Against such, there is no law."* Jesus came to give us Abundant Life that overflows. The Abundant Life is a Supernatural Promise that He is referring to here. Happiness (The World's version of Joy) is something that you have to pay to get. People can have everything in the World and will be happy for only 5 minutes. They always want more. They never have joy that satisfies them and brings contentment. Joy is free, and you can be dead broke and have it overflowing in your life. Jesus said out of your belly will flow rivers of living water John 7:38, *"He that believeth on me, as the Scripture hath said, out of his belly shall flow rivers of living water."* Joy is obeying the Lord and experiencing the Fruits of the Spirit.

We have a Mighty River inside of us that wants to overflow. This River is the Spirit of God. When we submit to and follow God, then the Spirit of God inside of us starts to burst like a 2-liter coke bottle with several Mentos dropped in it! YouTube it if you haven't seen this. It is an explosive overflowing and nothing can contain it. When this happens, we experience supernatural things that the World cannot comprehend, and we are blown away. We can be drunk in the Spirit at 9 am (Acts 2) and still be ok to drive. I am telling you that if you have not experienced this, then you are missing out. Jesus wants us to have fun with the supernatural things He provides for us, not the worldly stuff that brings a hangover. There is Joy in serving the Lord. Ephesians 5:17-19 says,

> *"Therefore, do not be foolish, but understand what the Lord's will is. Do not get drunk on wine, which leads to debauchery. Instead, be filled with the Spirit, speaking to one another with psalms, hymns, and songs from the Spirit. Sing and make music from your heart to the Lord."*

So, don't get drunk, which leads to sin but be filled with the Spirit. Talk about the Lord and sing songs to the Lord. This brings you Joy rather than only temporary happiness. God will put a song in your heart that will lift you out of any despair.

So how do you get filled with the Spirit? That's a good question. I will give you some ways to be filled with the Spirit. Being filled means first, we need to empty out something. If we want to be all the way filled with God, then we need to empty all the worldly things out of our temple first. Then we can be entirely filled with God. Therefore, if you have sin in your life, then you must repent and confess this sin. You have to start walking with the Lord and spending time with Him. The Holy Spirit within us needs to connect with God to refuel and overflow. So, you can get the picture, I will say that we are the 2-liter coke bottle, and Jesus is the Mentos. We need to go to Jesus so He can drop that sweet, sweet Mentos into us so we can explode with supernatural Love, Joy, Peace, Patience, Goodness, Gentleness, Meekness, and Self-Control. If we are full of offense and bitterness regularly and we try to get filled with the Spirit, then we are fooling ourselves, and our prayers don't go past the ceiling Matthew 5:23-24,

> *"So, if you are offering your gift at the altar and there remember that your brother has something against you, leave your gift there before the altar and go. First, be reconciled to your brother, and then come and offer your gift."*

God wants you to have peace with your brother in your heart and theirs, if possible. Be the first to forgive. Be set free from the trap of the enemy. Do not let that unforgiveness take root because it will affect your prayer life.

God wants you to be pure in your heart and mind so you can be filled with the Holy Spirit daily. This is not a once a week activity like Church. Give us this day our Daily Bread, not weekly or monthly, or just holiday bread. We need to be at the place where God is our Bread that we depend on for sustenance. If you are using other things to satisfy you, you are filled with those things, and they will just leave you feeling empty and needing more. Jesus said out of your belly will flow Rivers of Living Water. This refreshing River causes everything to flourish. It takes obedience to have a close walk with the Lord, but I can testify that it is AWESOME! I know plenty of Christians, but they do not have a close supernatural walk with the Lord. They go through the motions doing religious things but are not having a Mentos reaction. This is because they are full of themselves and other evil worldly things. We must search within ourselves and have the Holy Spirit shine the Light on every area that needs to be cleared out and given to God.

Now when your life is on point in the Lord, you can start having truly unique supernatural experiences. People will see the Fruit of the Spirit in your life and want to drop those stupid, sinful habits that just weigh them down and are oppressive. Freedom in Christ is just the beginning of Joy. Therefore, when you want to have an overflow in the Spirit, you should be doing several things as a lifestyle change. The five big ones for me are reading the Word of God, daily devotionals, prayer, worship, and ministry. These five things are vital to living an Abundant Life and being filled with the Spirit. God speaks to us like a GPS, and we need to learn to start taking turn-by-turn directions.

We are to wash our minds daily with the Word of God to renew our minds. I expect God to show me what I need to do that day for Him, as well. Let's say I read a passage of Scripture on forgiveness that day. Then I am on the lookout for the opportunity to show grace to someone and forgive them for something they are going to do to me. If the passage is about serving, I will ask the Lord whom He wants me to serve that day. God does not want us to read the Word of God, and it be a random experience. He is in control and will show us what He wants us to read, and the Words will rise out of the page and slap us in the face in a good way. This is called a Rhema Word from God. You will start reading the Logos Word of God (Written form), and the Rhema Word (God's Spirit Spoken Word) will literally speak to you. God will give you an Instant Word at that moment from His Written Word.

I have several daily devotionals that I bought that are topical. I have a daily devotional with 365 topics. I turn to the day's date, and it has Scriptures and a subject to apply to my day. The Lord will surely guide me and warn me what to look out for at the same time. The Logos Word of God will also become a Rhema Word of God as you read it in a devotional. The same occurs when you hear a Pastor preaching or someone talking about certain Scriptures. These are confirmations from the Holy Spirit that guide you in your life. God is alive, and He is speaking to us daily. God wants to speak to us every day intimately, and the Rhema Word of God is a superb way that He does it.

You will start to see the Hand of the Lord in the daily reading of His Word and devotionals, and it will bring you Joy knowing that God cares enough to speak to You. The Creator of this Universe wants to sit next to you and open His Word to you. It is amazing. Get ready for the Holy Spirit to illuminate the Word and bring Joy into your life. John 8:31-32 says, "*Then Jesus said to those Jews who believed Him, "If you abide in My Word, you are My disciples indeed. And you shall know the truth, and the truth shall make you free.*" You have to abide in His Word so you can be a disciple of Jesus. If you are a true disciple that stays in the Word and obeys It, you shall know the Truth, and when you apply It, It will set you free! Freedom brings Joy. Ask someone who gets out of prison if they feel worse being free?

Prayer can be perceived as many different things in the Bible, but ultimately it is talking to God. Prayer is how Jesus said we should be giving honor to God Matthew 6:8-14 says,

"For your Father knows the things you have need of before you ask Him. In this manner, therefore, pray: Our Father in Heaven, Hallowed be Your name. Your Kingdom come, Your Will be done On earth, as it is in Heaven. Give us this day our daily Bread. And forgive us our sins, As we forgive those, who have sinned against us. And do not lead us into temptation, But deliver us from the evil one. For Yours is the kingdom and the power and the glory forever. Amen "For if you forgive men their trespasses, your heavenly Father will also forgive you. But if you do not forgive men their trespasses, neither will your Father forgive your trespasses."

Prayer needs are something that God already knows that you need before you ask Him. God already knows what you are going to pray. Therefore, Jesus said when you pray; don't just get right to what you want but first honor God by saying, "Your Name be glorified!" Prayer should start with you, praising God and telling Him how Awesome He is asking for His Kingdom to come and His Will to be done. If you pray according to God's Will, He hears you, and you will have the petition you prayed about answered. When we pray for God's Kingdom to come in our lives, then we want order and Power to flow. Order comes from obeying God in Heaven and submitting to Him. Then His Power from on High to enrich our lives will be evident and active. We have to ask Him to give us our supernatural Bread for the day. We are in receiving mode at this point. We are being filled with the Spirit because we are lifting up the Name of Jesus and praising Him.

The Bible says we should ask God to forgive us of our sins "AS" we forgive others. Jesus wants us to reconcile with each other and live in peace and harmony without contentions and strife with bitterness. Your mouth will give you away. If you have anything evil in your heart throughout the day, listen to what you say and the way that you say it, Ephesians 4:29 says, "*Let no corrupt communication proceed out of your mouth, but that which is good to the use of edifying, that it may minister grace unto the hearers.*" God cannot fill us and let His Forgiving Love flow through us if we do not forgive others. We hold onto that unforgiveness like an evil zombie dog with a bone and are filled with hate. We cannot be filled with hate and love at the same time.

You must choose 1 John 4:21 says, "*And this commandment we have from Him: that he who loves God must love his brother also.*" We should pray not to be led into temptation but delivered from Satan. We end with praising God again. Prayer is a victorious mindset to have. Praise God in the beginning and Praise Him at the end. God is not evil and won't give us a snake (Luke 11:11). Pray and ask what you need, and don't expect bad things from God. Expect good things and have faith in God. Pray and ask by faith because without faith it is impossible to please God on any level.

Prayer is also listening to God. When we pray, we are to give God our worries and doubts, along with our fears. We are to ask for forgiveness and receive that forgiveness. When it comes to unforgiveness, prayer is like taking out the trash. The Devil wants us to get offended and form a Contract of Wrath. We must dispose of that trash. God will take it away if we allow Him to take it. When you are taking out the trash it is best to do it right before the trash man comes so you do not have to deal with the stink of letting that trash just sit around. When we do not pray right away to get rid of that offense the enemy will spew all of his rotten schemes in our ear until we take out the trash. Good thing God doesn't just come once or twice a week to take out the trash! He shows up to take out the trash immediately while we are praying. I wish the regular trash guy could come like that to get the garbage!

When we are done talking to God and getting what is on our hearts out in the open, then it is time to let God speak to us. Just like with any relationship, one person speaks the other person listens. If you want to know God more and have a supernatural understanding and the Fruits of the Spirit in your life, then it all starts here. Listen to God. Start with one minute and listen to God. When I first started doing this, I remember hearing a voice telling me to order pizza for a whole minute. I had to fine-tune my ears to filter out my fleshly voice. Oh, and when you start doing this, the enemy will be furious.

The enemy will distract you with your phone ringing (it should be on silent, so you aren't distracted, rookie mistake!) with someone knocking on the door or with anything you have allowed him to use. We must prepare to seek the Lord and make sure that we have taken the proper measures to have a breakthrough with God. If you have a dog that needs to be fed or walked, don't pray first. The dog will bark and growl, trying to go outside or be fed, and your prayers will be hindered. Plan your time with the Lord. If you are married, go and tell your spouse you are going to pray, and everything else must wait. The enemy will use anything you allow him to, so be prepared. Planning to minimize distractions shows God you are serious, and He will reward you for this.

Listening to God can be a tricky thing. We have to fine-tune our ears to hear the Voice of God. He may want to give you a specific Scripture for that moment. He may tell you He wants you to pray for a friend. He may want to tell you about something He wants you to do in your life. He will talk to you personally. Discern the Voice of the Lord and obey it 1 Samuel 3:1-10 says Samuel had to learn to hear God,

"The boy Samuel ministered before the Lord under Eli. In those days, the Word of the Lord was rare; there were not many visions. One night Eli, whose eyes were becoming so weak that he could barely see, was lying down in his usual place. The lamp of God had not yet gone out, and Samuel was lying down in the house of the Lord, where the ark of God was. Then the Lord called Samuel.

Samuel answered, "Here I am." And he ran to Eli and said, "Here I am; you called me." But Eli said, "I did not call; go back and lie down." So he went and lay down. Again the Lord called, "Samuel!" And Samuel got up and went to Eli and said, "Here I am; you called me." My son," Eli said, "I did not call; go back and lie down." Now Samuel did not yet know the Lord: The Word of the Lord had not yet been revealed to him. A third time, the Lord called, "Samuel!" And Samuel got up and went to Eli and said, "Here I am; you called me." Then Eli realized that the Lord was calling the boy. So Eli told Samuel, "Go and lie down, and if he calls you, say, 'Speak, Lord, for your servant is listening.'" So Samuel went and lay down in his place. The Lord came and stood there, calling as at the other times, "Samuel! Samuel!" Then Samuel said, "Speak, for your servant is listening." And the Lord spoke to Samuel."

Samuel was a young Prophet of God, and He did not know God was speaking to Him. He ran to Eli three different times. Nevertheless, Samuel thought it was the voice of a friend. It was God. You will get it wrong sometimes, and that is ok. It takes practice to hear the Voice of God. However, Jesus said, "My Sheep know My Voice." We should take the time like Samuel, lie down, and listen for God's Voice no matter how long it takes. Now many times, I have listened and didn't hear anything. Nevertheless, the Lord was speaking to me through His Word and other things. Therefore, God is not silent, but maybe He just wanted to see how long I would lie still and focus to hear from Him. I am excited for you to start hearing from the Lord. It is incredible to have a close relationship with God.

Worship is another way to be filled with the Spirit. We can get into God's Presence at any time and worship Him allowing Him to fill us to overflowing. It is supernatural, and you have to practice just like listening to God in prayer. Christians in Non-Denominational services raise their hands during Worship. This is an outward sign of what is going on inside of their temple. They are surrendering to God in their hearts and getting ready to humble themselves by taking themselves off the throne. They are showing that they surrender and are not going to put up a fight. When you finally get to this place in worship, you can shut out the rest of the people in the room and focus on God as you do in prayer. Worship in a Church setting is full of people and possible distractions. It can be harder to enter into the Holy of Holies in worship at Church. You must be disciplined, or the three or four songs they sing will be over, and you never really reached the Throne Room. It is best to practice at home with a playlist of songs you like.

Praise and Worship is an excellent way to get close to the Lord. Many people do not practice both on a daily basis. Most Christians if they are going to Church only experience Praise and Worship for a few minutes before the service starts. If they are late for some reason then they miss out all together. Praise and Worship are together in a service but both are not always done in the service. My father always wanted to be on time for Praise and Worship and I never understood why. He said, "If I miss Praise and Worship I might as well just go back home!" There are other parts to the service but for Him Praise and Worship was very important. After being saved and having a personal relationship with the Lord I started to want to participate in Praise and Worship all the time.

Praise and Worship are two different things that are perceived to be only one. Many people will go to Church and hear music for a few minutes before service and feel that they successfully completed Praise and Worship. This is not the case at all. Praise and Worship in the Bible are two different things. It is not something that you can accomplish in only a few minutes before a service. Praise and Worship is a powerful and intimate supernatural experience. Praise and Worship is important for Spiritual Warfare, getting closer to God, and receiving revelation from God. However, it is called Praise and Worship. Praise should lead to worship, and it should be deep and meaningful.

Praise is described in the Bible as singing about the Lord. It is also singing praises to God. You are declaring things about God to Him. You are declaring your faith and beliefs about God in song. You are testifying about the Goodness of God. This brings you Joy as you shake off the negative mood you are in and get your mind off of yourself. We can have supernatural things broken off of us during Praise, Isaiah 61:3 says,

> *"To console those who mourn in Zion, To give them beauty for ashes, The oil of joy for mourning, The garment of praise for the spirit of heaviness; That they may be called trees of righteousness, The planting of the Lord, that He may be glorified."*

When we have a spirit of heaviness we can put on the garment of praise. When we praise God supernaturally we are allowing Him to break the spirit of heaviness off of us. 2 Corinthians 3:17 says, *"Now the Lord is the Spirit, and where the Spirit of the Lord is, there is freedom."*

When you feel the Presence of the Lord, He is bringing freedom to you. He is Powerful so if the enemy is attacking you by putting a spirit of heaviness and evil on you then the Holy Spirit will break it off of you when He shows up. Most people will get chill bumps, feel excited, and have peace. The Presence of God is Powerful and when we are going through something we need to Praise the Lord to get the victory. God shows up every time and He will deliver you if you trust in Him! Praise the Lord with all of your strength. Allow God to deliver you from the attack of the enemy! Don't hold back! Give it your all!

Before they went out to battle in the Old Testament, they would send the unarmed singers out first to declare victory by praising the Lord. Praise is how we can prepare for battle in 2 Chronicles 20:21-22,

> *"And when he had consulted with the people, he appointed those who should sing to the Lord, and who should praise the beauty of holiness, as they went out before the army and were saying: "Praise the Lord, For His mercy endures forever." Now when they began to sing and to praise, the Lord set ambushes against the people of Ammon, Moab, and Mount Seir, who had come against Judah; and they were defeated."*

These singers declared, "Praise the Lord, for His Mercy endures forever." This is a testimony about the Mercy of God. They had seen the Mercy of God and appreciated it. They knew God would deliver them because He has done it before. They were encouraged by Praising God and then God responded by defeating their enemy.

Praising God gets you into a victorious mindset. It helps you to remember the attributes of God and who He is. We are to enter into His Presence with thanksgiving as it says in Psalms 100:1-4,

> *"Make a joyful shout to the Lord, all you lands! Serve the Lord with gladness; Come before His presence with singing. Know that the Lord, He is God; It is He who has made us, and not we ourselves; We are His people and the sheep of His pasture. Enter into His gates with thanksgiving, And into His courts with praise. Be thankful to Him, and bless His name."*

It activates your faith and helps to renew your mind. It reminds you of what God has done for you in the past. This causes your Spirit to be renewed and you become filled with the Holy Spirit and faith. When you praise God your Spirit is awake and ready to serve the Lord. You are fired up and on a mission to get closer to God. When we sing about being grateful to God for what He has done it makes us want to Worship Him in a thankful and intimate way. This leads to worship.

Worship is where you sing to the Lord and are able to look into His Eyes and seek His Face. This is a huge revelation, so remember this. Worship is the doorway to receiving supernatural revelation from God. Worship is spending intimate time with God and reaching the Throne Room of Heaven. Worship is essential in spending time with God. Jesus said to worship in John 4:23-24,

"But the hour is coming, and now is, when the true worshipers will worship the Father in Spirit and truth, for the Father is seeking such to worship Him. God is Spirit, and those who worship Him must worship in Spirit and truth."

People miss out on Divine Revelation and impartation because they do not know about Worship. They miss out by praising God a lot and being energetic, clapping their hands and dancing, which has its place. Psalms 95:6 says, "*O come, let us worship and bow down: let us kneel before the Lord, our maker.*"

The Holy Spirit wants to do a work in our lives, and this is a significant way He does it. It's as if He is performing surgery on us and removing impurities out of us. The Presence of the Lord is a refining fire Malachi 3:2, "*But who can endure the day of His coming? And who can stand when He appears? For He is like a refiner's fire and like launderers' soap.*" The refiner has to heat the metal so the metal can give up the impurities that were hidden in the metal. This process takes time, but once the metal yields its impurities, the refiner can remove them, and the metal is pure.

Worship in Hebrew is proskuneo, which means to worship or lie prostrate in worship. We are not only to put our hands up or kneel but also to lay down prostrate. Prostrate means lying stretched out on the ground with one's face downward. This is the act of worship in the Hebrew. So, when you worship the Lord or see someone else worship the Lord, Biblically, it could mean raising your hands, kneeling, bowing, or laying on your belly with outstretched arms and your face on the floor. It is an outward expression of genuine respect and reverence of the Lord Psalm 29:2, "*Give unto the Lord the glory due unto his name; worship the Lord in the beauty of holiness.*" When we are deep in worship and intimately seeking the Lord we find beauty in His Holiness. He wants to reveal Himself to us and is inviting us to draw near to Him. When we surrender to the Lord in Worship we see a side of the Lord that is beautiful and intimate. Only through worship can we have this special revelation. It reminds me of how Jesus transfigured before the disciples in Matthew 17:1-2 says,

> "*Now after six days Jesus took Peter, James, and John his brother, led them up on a high mountain by themselves; and He was transfigured before them. His face shone like the sun, and His clothes became as white as the light.*"

God is always revealing something new to us and it never gets boring. He is Awesome! Worship keeps us heavenly-minded Isaiah 26:3, "*You will keep him in perfect peace, whose mind is stayed on You Because he trusts in You.*" We learn to trust God as we spend time with Him. We have to focus our mind and keep it locked on Him to continually be filled with the Spirit. What a revelation. God will pour out His Spirit if you are willing! There is never a dry eye in the house when you are truly worshiping the Lord. When you are in His Presence, you feel Freedom and Love. Peace and Joy are always flowing from the Lord in Worship. However, you have to break through all of your preconceived ideas and sinful mindsets to have this experience. God is a rewarder of those that diligently seek Him. It's not about a specific Religion; it's about a close personal Biblical relationship. We have to be genuine when we approach God. He wants an open and honest relationship with you.

When you worship it is a time of focus and intimacy. Worship music is normally slower. You are able to calm down from the quick tempo of Praise music and focus on seeking the Face of God. When I am worshiping I have my eyes closed and my hands raised. When I am at home I am comfortable and lying on my back with my hands in the air. The Lord wants us to be comfortable and not having our blood flow cut off to our legs so it tingles and we cannot walk. I have been there and it is ok. Do whatever the Lord leads you to do in the situation that you are in. When you get comfortable and block out all distractions you can focus on the Lord. You can be transcended into the Presence of God and it is miraculous.

When you are focused on God, He will take you out of your "fleshly mindset" into His Direct Presence. Once you are in His Presence, time stands still and you are in awe of Him. I encourage you to do everything in your power to get away from distractions and worship the Lord intimately without the restrictions of time. Worshiping in a Church service is Awesome but when you grow into maturity you will crave the Presence of God and it will be a priority for you. It's like Superman getting direct sunlight to get recharged for battle. We as Christians need this like oxygen. I challenge you to get to know the Lord in the Beauty of His Holiness. A mature Christian understands how to be a Warrior and a Worshiper. Now that you have this knowledge it is up to you to surrender to the call of the Lord to Worship!

Keeping worship music going in our vehicles and our homes is vital. We should be able to walk into a room even if we are having a bad day and hear worship music playing. This will motivate us to surrender to the Spirit and get right into worship. This will give us victory over our flesh and the enemy who is trying to distract us. I can't tell you how many times I've been getting tempted by the Devil or in a spiritual battle and then walk into my bedroom and hear worship music playing. It is such a joy to be able to walk into a room and feel the Presence of the Lord because it puts things into perspective for me. I know that at that moment, I can just go to the Lord and have Him lift all these burdens off of me and receive His Peace and Victory through His Presence. At any point in time, you should be able to stop and worship the Lord and gain victory over the enemy when he attacks you. Our sanity is found in Christ Jesus. We don't have to wait until Sunday to be filled with God. He is available anytime, and He is not like the DMV that has a long line.

Ministry is another way to be filled with the Holy Spirit, and we have talked about this before. When you are helping others, God will pour His Spirit out on you, and you will be filled while you are ministering to others. God allows you to overflow in the Spirit and not just be filled. It is a privilege to work for the Lord and to be used for His Kingdom. The Gifts of the Spirit start flowing as He wills them to, and anything is possible. Ministry is not always something that will cause you to be filled with Joy constantly. The Devil likes to give us a hard time, be filled with the Spirit before ministering.

One night, I remember holding a Bible study and having a few couples from the Church over to the house. After the Bible study, I really wanted to pray and just go to bed. I was tired from a long day at Bible College and then working a full shift. I wanted to just go to bed because I had the same schedule the next day. Someone in the group who was new to the faith wanted to be prayed for with anointing oil. I knew I was not feeling supercharged with faith because I was so tired. I told everyone to pray in the Spirit so we could call on God to show up. As soon as I prayed for her, she fell out. The Anointing of God fell on me like a thick cloud. I felt like I was in the Armor of God and I had put on my helmet and shut the face plate of the helmet down over my face. I lost my identity. God ministered to everyone there. They all had fallen out in the Spirit or had a touch from God and demons were cast out. Afterward, I felt like a warrior on the battlefield that had slain all of the enemies and was standing victorious. I heard a voice say, "You are a God, Paul." I immediately knew the Devil was trying to tempt with pride.

We are nothing but dust. God has put His Treasure in these earthen vessels, so He gets the Glory. The first rule of ministry is that you should never minister in your own strength! God stopped Gideon from using a whole army because he wanted the Glory. He had Gideon whittle his army down to only 300 men against an army that was vast. God wanted there to be no confusion as to who was really fighting the battle. God got the Glory, so Gideon could not brag about his strength. The Abundant Life is a Blessing, and it is real. Let's pray and ask God to give us the Abundant Life He promises.

Pray this prayer out loud. "Heavenly Father, thank You for Your Son Jesus, Who promised that I could have an Abundant Life. I thank You for my salvation. I ask You to forgive me of my sins that have hindered me from walking closely with You. I want to walk with You and experience Joy! Lord, help me to serve You in all that I do. Help me to walk by faith and believe Your Word. Help me to walk on water and believe You for miracles. Help me to enjoy Your Presence and to worship You always. Lord please put a song in my heart and fill me with Joy as I praise You. Lord, I need more of You. Holy Spirit, please fill me. I accept Your Outpouring in my life. Help me to walk closer with You. I make You Lord of my life. In Jesus Name I pray. Amen."

CHAPTER 13

Practical Spiritual Warfare

"So Jesus answered and said to them, Assuredly, I say to you, if you have faith and do not doubt, you will not only do what was done to the fig tree, but also if you say to this mountain, Be removed and be cast into the sea, it will be done." Matthew 21:21

Never feel stupid to rebuke the enemy. You may feel something happening to your body, and you do not think it is demonic, so you don't do anything. However, the enemy will keep oppressing you, whether it is thoughts or a symptom in your body. Rebuke it, and if it is demonic, it will stop. Take authority because your body is subject to the Authority of God as well. Therefore, it will line up. Faith, without doubt, is what the Lord wants us to have. I believe that doubt is logical. If you have faith but are still thinking logically, then you will cancel out any faith you had. Peter looked down and saw the logic of what was happening and fell into the logical truth and laws that govern this World. This is why the Bible says that we walk by faith and not by sight. Sight is one of the five senses, and all of your senses will point toward logic. Think about it! Faith always defies logic. Choose faith and watch miracles happen! There is a famous saying, which is, "You can doubt and do without." This is not God's Plan for an Abundant Life. The Heroes of the Bible had logic problems, but God helped them move past it to God's supernatural realm of faith. They did the impossible, and they cast mountains into the sea after they believed and threw logic aside.

<u>Voices</u>

We are fighting an invisible enemy. We have voices in our heads that are sometimes hard to discern. I encourage you to practice writing down the thoughts that you have daily in a journal. Write down what voice you think is speaking to you. It could be the Devil, it could be God, or it could be your flesh. Pray about this and ask God to help you to discern the voices. This is very practical and will help you to find out who is speaking to you. In the Old Testament, Samuel had to lie still, concentrate, and listen to the voice that was talking to him. He didn't understand that it was the Lord that was speaking to him. He thought it was the voice of someone close to him. Therefore, we can see that when the Lord speaks to us, it is in a friendly Voice. It's a familiar Voice that we can understand. It's a Voice that we want to listen to and trust.

When we hear the voices in our heads, we can start to listen to them, and sometimes we know right away what voice is speaking to us. Sometimes we don't know or just ignore them. In this case, I would write down what that voice is telling you and ask a Christian you trust. They may be able to help you discern which voices are speaking to you. Another way is to go and check the Bible. See if that phrase is in the Bible or if there is a similar voice or Scripture in the Bible that resembles the statement that was spoken to you. It is vital to weed out the voices that are speaking to us because it is a Biblical mandate that we are responsible for doing. The Bible says that we are supposed to take captive the thoughts that are entering into our minds.

It is imperative to understand who is talking to you. The Devil wants to confuse you and discourage you. He wants you to give up, and he wants you to give in to the flesh. He doesn't want you to serve God. When the enemy speaks to you, and you listen to him, his evil anointing comes over you. It makes you discouraged and feel like you are filthy and unworthy. When we listen to what the Devil says to us, it taints our mind to where we cannot think. We get confused, disoriented, and discouraged. When we listen to the enemy, it drives us further toward him and away from God. The enemy wants us to worship him and to do what he says. The way the enemy speaks to you always encourages you to think there's something wrong. It causes you to doubt and to be unstable. When the Lord speaks to you, He brings encouragement and confidence. Even the chastening of the Lord brings Peace.

Knowing who is speaking to you is just the beginning of warfare. When we start to take the voice captive to the obedience of Christ, then we have a fight on our hands. The Devil does not want you to give him any lip or fight back at all. The Devil will challenge your authority and your identity. Fighting the enemy is an everyday battle. The Devil will try to bombard our minds. The Devil will try to make you feel like you're going insane. He will confuse you, discourage you, and overwhelm you with evil thoughts. He will try to make you think that you have addictions, and he will tell you there's no way out. He will overrun your mind with thoughts if you don't rebuke him daily. Sometimes you have to rebuke him several times an hour. If you are not rebuking the enemy, then you are accepting his doctrine and lies. This means you are slowly forming another contract with him. Fighting the enemy, according to the Bible, is a daily chore. We have the victory if we choose to fight the battle. Many Christians will not fight the good fight of faith because they get complacent. They become defeated and overwhelmed. We have to make sure that we are being encouraged and being filled with the Spirit continually. The days of just going to Church once a week are over. The real Christian walk is a daily walk and a minute-by-minute real-time relationship with Jesus Christ. There is no lag in our relationship with Jesus Christ. His connection with us is strong, and there are no restrictions on it.

Rebuking the enemy is our job as a Christian. We are not to let the enemy come through our walls or gates of our city. Proverbs 25:28 says, "*Whoever has no rule over his own spirit Is like a city broken down, without walls.*" We are to make sure that we are guarding the walls of our temple through submitting to God and the Power of the Holy Spirit. The enemy tries to come through our minds with thoughts. This is why we are talking about thoughts as practical spiritual warfare. If you let the enemy tell you whatever he wants to and don't rebuke him, you will let him take over your mind. You have to have control of your mind. If not, then you are like a city that's broken down without walls. You must be in control of your temple, which includes your mind. When you take control of your mind through the Holy Spirit's Power, you will be successful in rebuking the enemy.

Satan will try to get you off guard. It reminds me of the Guardsman in England that sits in front of the Royal Palace. Satan is like that person who keeps on annoying the Guard, trying to break his concentration. You see people on videos trying to make the Guard laugh or smile. They also try to get the Guard to flinch or react to what they're doing. The Guard is not a civilian, and he has enlisted into a Royal Army. He is not to act like a civilian or let civilians disrupt the mission that he is on. It is the same way for us as Christians. We are in the Lord's army, and he has put us on a specific assignment. He does not want us to break that assignment. He tells us not to be like the World and not to do what they do. We cannot allow the enemy to distract us. If we compromise in the smallest area of our lives, then we will break our concentration of serving God.

If the Guardsman is on a post, they are to serve that post seriously. They are not to be influenced by the civilians trying to distract them. They can be docked pay if they are caught slipping or laughing. They can ultimately get removed from the Guard if their infraction is severe enough. The person trying to get them to be distracted is trying to get them in trouble or fired. Maybe this person is unaware of the consequences of their actions, but they do it, nonetheless. The Devil is strategic in his planning to get us to slip up while on duty. If we understand that being a soldier is a serious business and a calling, we are less likely to be distracted by the enemy's ploy or with temptations. Nevertheless, we are human. "We can't be perfect, so why bother if Christianity demands perfection?" No! These are half-truths and must be disputed by you knowing and using the Word of God!

Your relationship with Jesus is serious. You are a soldier in an Army that is being killed and persecuted daily. The enemy hates you and is trying to get you to compromise so he can ruin your life. He is continuously trying to distract you and get you to sin. All the Devil needs to do is to distract you. If he can get you to look into any sin long enough and convince you that it is ok to compromise just this one time, then he has you. Christianity isn't about rules and regulations. It's about a relationship with Jesus Christ. This relationship is unique, and God expects things from us. There are consequences when we do not stay close to the Lord. God will allow you to be distracted by the enemy. When we sin like the guard, we will be punished. God does not punish us the same way whenever we sin. When we sin, we are separating ourselves from a close relationship with Jesus. We know that when we choose to sin, we are choosing to step away from the Lord. The more we sin, the more steps we take away from the Lord.

Practical spiritual warfare is also removing sin from our lives. I am not trying to tell you that you can never sin again. You can always sin, but there will always be consequences. The consequences are never the same. You could go and sleep with a person, feel guilty, confess, and repent to God, and that is all that happens. You could sin by sleeping with someone, and then you catch HIV. You could get this consequence on the first time you do it or on the second time that you do it. We never know what the consequences of sin are going to be. However, spiritually speaking, every time we sin, we create a space between God and us. We allow sin to come between God and us. This sin can become an idol. We begin to worship sin instead of God. Something is an idol to you if you can't stop doing it or thinking about it. Sinning requires commitment. You have to think about it, rationalize it, and justify doing it. Once you commit to doing sin, then it is hard not to sin. The Lord gives us a way out of sinning during the temptation. Once we have made up our mind to sin, we have chosen not to take the way out that the Lord has given us. We can escape the temptation 1 Corinthians 10:13 says,

> *"No temptation has overtaken you except such as is common to man; but God is faithful, who will not allow you to be tempted beyond what you are able, but with the temptation will also make the way of escape, that you may be able to bear it."*

Once we remove habitual sin out of our lives, we will silence the voice of the controlling enemy. The enemy is no longer able to control us. He is only allowed to tempt us to sin and oppress us. Practical spiritual warfare at this point is to keep your mind stayed on Jesus. Isaiah 26:3 says, "*I will keep you in perfect peace if your mind stays on me because he trusts me.*" We are always supposed to have the Mind of Christ. Paul says if there's anything good, heavenly, or pure, think on these things. Our mind is to be focused on the things of God. It's good to continually be in a relationship with Jesus so you can talk to Him all day long. This is what Paul says, when he mentions always praying without ceasing. That simply means to be praying to God in talking to God all day long. It means to have a continuous relationship with Him and not just to pray once in the morning or evening. Those prayers turn into just asking for forgiveness. If we keep an open relationship with the Lord, He is continually speaking to us and warning us about the enemy trying to tempt us, and we can bring these temptations and thoughts captive to Him in real-time. I have spoken to you about worship and being filled with the Spirit. If you are filled with the Holy Spirit, you will not fulfill the lusts of the flesh.

When we put on the Armor of God, it is not so we can just be on the defensive all the time. The Sword of the Spirit is the Word of God, and it is our offensive Weapon. You want to make sure that you are quoting Scripture to the enemy whenever he speaks to you (Matthew 4:10). If the Devil tells you that you are going to die today, you can rebuke him by quoting Scripture to him. You can say to him that no weapon formed against you will prosper (Isaiah 54:17). The Devil is a liar, but you need to tell him that he is a liar. You need to speak out loud what you believe on the inside. You need to use the Word of God against him. He will not leave you alone until he sees that you are serious. The fight is continuous.

The Devil must be confronted with God's Word and faith; otherwise, he will just take over your mind and your temple. We have been given authority over the enemy by Jesus. Mark 16:15-17 says,

"And He said to them, "Go into all the world and preach the Gospel to every creature. He who believes and is baptized will be saved, but he who does not believe will be condemned. And these signs will follow those who believe: In My Name, they will cast out demons."

Jesus told His Disciples that they were to fulfill the Great Commission. He said whoever believes in My Name they will cast out demons. Therefore, this means not only the Apostles who were preaching the Gospel would have these abilities, but also future believers. That means for us today that we have authority over the enemy. Our Power in Christ is real, and the beginning stage of the enemy attacking us begins in our minds. Rebuke the enemy and put him in his place. I usually tell Satan to shut up, leave, and go back to the pit of hell. It is essential to tell the enemy to shut up, so he quits talking. Give him direction and make him leave. The Devil is a master of deception, so you do not want him to keep talking because he will lead you astray.

Bible Interpretation

It is crucial to understand how to interpret the Bible. If you are saved, then you have the same Holy Spirit in you that inspired the authors who wrote It. The Holy Spirit will lead you to the Truth. It is up to us to listen to the Holy Spirit, who gently speaks to us and surrender to His Voice. To correctly interpret the Bible, you must understand many different important interpretation rules. When trying to understand a Scripture in the Bible, you have to know the author's identity and original audience of that Book in the Bible. Once you figure this out, then you need to identify the original message the author was conveying to that audience. Once you get the original message, then you can try to see if it is applicable to us today. The Scripture you are looking up must be read in context so you can fully understand the author's message and meaning. You have to realize that the Book of the Bible you are reading was written as a letter that was meant to be read all at once. It can be understood easier by reading the entire Book or Chapter. This will give you the overall tone or message of the Book or Chapter. Then if you want to study one passage of Scripture in that Chapter, you will not misinterpret it as easily.

Let us look at a famous passage to see how to interpret it correctly, John 3:16, "_For God so loved the world that He gave His only begotten Son, that whoever believes in Him should not perish but have everlasting life._" Now the original author was John, and it is believed that he wrote it in Ephesus in the year 80 A.D. He wrote it to a general audience, which includes Jews and Gentiles. Gentiles are any other people groups outside of the Jewish race. If you were reading the Book of Matthew, the author wrote to a Jewish audience, so it has many phrases that are not easily understood without studying early Jewish culture. In the Book of John, the message in John 3:16 is for any person who reads it. This is understood when John says, "Whoever believes in Him." Therefore, you can take that message from this Scripture and apply it to your life today. It is an open invitation for anyone who hears the news and believes then they can be saved.

The Scripture starts out with saying God loved the World (Humans) so much that He gave His Son (Jesus) and whoever (Anyone) believes (Accepts and Trusts) in Him will not perish (Go to Hell) but have everlasting life (Be saved and go to Heaven). I gave some examples of correct interpretation but know that the Bible interprets the Bible. You have to allow the whole Bible to speak to and help interpret any Scripture you are reading. The Bible will not contradict Itself, so it only helps you understand It better if you reference other Scriptures similar to the passage you are studying. For instance, Romans 5:8 references the Scripture above, "_But God demonstrates His own love toward us, in that while we were still sinners, Christ died for us._" Scripture helps to interpret and understand Scripture. Most study Bibles will have a reference guide in the middle or side of each page of the Bible that shows you which Scriptures reference each other. It is a helpful tool to understand the Bible more clearly.

If you have a study Bible, then you are way ahead of the average Christian. It gives you references of almost every Scripture in the Bible to help you easily understand the Scripture you are looking to interpret. It will provide you with the background info of the Book itself, including identifying the author, historical background, message, and purpose of the Book. It will also give you maps, glossaries, definitions, and many other exciting tools that will help you rightly divide the Word of Truth. If you have a regular Bible, then I highly encourage you to upgrade immediately. The Word of God is your Weapon, so you need to make sure that you have the best Weapon available and sharpen It daily. You see, reading the Word is great, but when you properly understand It, memorize It, and apply It in your life, then It becomes the Sword of the Spirit. This Weapon will be effective in defeating the enemy, and the Devil is scared of any Christian that wields this Sword!

There are two types of ways to interpret the Bible one is Biblical, and another is not. The first is Exegesis. This is the proper way to study the Bible by excavating or digging down to the original message and then properly applying it to us today. The second method is Eisegesis, and it is when someone ignores the rules of proper interpretation and tries to interpret the Scriptures based on surface reading of the Scriptures. This type of interpretation leads to an improper understanding of the original message, and the reader can twist the Word of God to mean anything they want.

Let us look at Matthew 7:1 about judging people, "_Judge not, that you be not judged._" If you ignore all interpretation rules and just try to find a meaning on the surface, you might come up with a few different meanings. One could be that you should not judge people. Another would be don't judge people, and God will not judge you. Therefore, if this was accurate, we could avoid God's judgment by not judging other people. Therefore, we could go to Heaven by not judging other people. You may get another meaning based on your perception of the words in that phrase based on your life experiences, worldview, and emotions.

When you read this Scripture in context, you will see that the Bible says that we should work on our own problems and repent before we try to judge other people hypocritically. We are to judge sin but not people, that is God's Job. We are to judge prophecy, spirits, sin, and other things. The enemy will use incorrect interpretations to misguide us and cause us to believe demonic doctrines. This one misinterpretation could possibly promote us to never judge anyone because the Bible says not to judge. Therefore, this gives a person the right to do whatever they want. If you speak up or tell them they are wrong, you judge them, and you appear to be the enemy. The Word of God is Powerful, and its correct interpretation is vital.

New theologies and countless Religions have been formed based on misinterpretations. They cannot be disproven because the founder is dead, and the followers are die-hard believers and will not listen to Absolute Truth. You must pray for the people who are deceived and help them divide God's Word rightly. People grow up in certain Religions and can have generational allegiances. They will fight against the Truth and anyone who preaches the Truth because they feel like you may be threatening their family's intelligence or traditions. They start to defend their family's beliefs regardless of the Truth. Some people would rather believe a lie than betray their family. The Truth is more important than past belief systems, no matter who started them. Doctrine is based on the interpretation of certain Scriptures. Religions practice doctrine. You must find out what doctrines your Church practices and believes. Their doctrines may not be Biblical, that will affect your theology and walk with God. People create doctrines based on half-truths, be very careful.

Be in Good Health

Sleeping is crucial in having spiritual victory. If you are running on one hour of sleep a day, you will be very irritable and easily distracted by the enemy. The Devil loves to get us moody, so we aren't focused on fighting him or spending time with God. We should never go too long without sleeping, too long without eating, or too long without praying. All of these things will lead us to want to sin. There is a Snickers commercial where a person is whining, crying, and acting crazy. His friends told him to have a Snickers because he wasn't acting like himself. Once he had a bite of Snickers, he was normal again. This commercial is funny because once we get hungry, we become irritable, and that's all we can think about is food. Our body is trying to tell us that we need nourishment and sustenance to function correctly. God wants us to eat food, so we need to make sure that we do it when we need to, and it is healthy food. Now, if the Lord is telling you to fast, then study fasting and choose what you want to do. Every fast is different, and we should rely on the Lord to show us what to do.

When serving the Lord, we need to make sure that we are sober. The Bible says to be sober-minded because your enemy, the Devil comes around like a roaring lion seeking whom he may devour. It is hard enough to fight the enemy and deal with the problems of this World when you are sober. If you are not sober, then the enemy will have a field day with you. If you aren't sober, you don't want to have an intimate walk with the Lord. I have talked to people who have been drunk or high and say that they had an incredible experience with the Lord. However, once they sober up, they realized that this perception was a deception. Having an intimate relationship with the Lord requires sobriety. In my opinion, this includes caffeine. I drank caffeine for years. I remember waking up, and coffee was the first thought in my mind. It motivated me to get out of bed sometimes. It became an idol for me. I remember having caffeine and being in Sunday worship and hitting a brick wall. I wanted to get closer to the Lord in worship, but it's as if the caffeine effects were blocking me from being intimate with the Lord on a deeper level. It's as if God put up a wall and wouldn't let me get past it until I was sober. I realized that I needed to get more intimate with the Lord but at a time when I was more vulnerable. The Lord wanted me to be sober, and for me, that included caffeine. If the Lord reveals anything as a possible idol, then it is best not to argue with the Lord and just discard it. If it is not easily discarded, then it is definitely an idol.

<u>Anointing Oil</u>

Anointing Oil is also a powerful tool to have. The Bible says that if you are sick, you should go to the elders and have them anoint you with oil and the prayer of faith will save the sick. Using oil that is anointed can help elevate your faith. I use Anointing Oil to pray over people, my house, my possessions, and myself. The Anointing in the New Testament is transferable to objects as well. Paul had a handkerchief that was Anointed, and God will use Anointing Oil as well. It's crucial to anoint yourself and others in prayer. Using Anointing Oil is Biblical, and the Holy Spirit honors it when we use it by faith.

Anointing Oil is used as a point of contact for faith. It is a symbol of the Holy Spirit. Anointing Oil was used in the Old Testament as a symbol of God choosing someone for a special purpose. In the New Testament we are to use it as a blessing of God's Presence in our lives. It marks someone or something to be ready for a visitation from the Lord. It takes faith to use Anointing Oil and it pleases the Lord when we have faith in Him. James 5 says that we are to call for the elders to be anointed in James 5:14-15, *"Is anyone among you sick? Let him call for the elders of the church, and let them pray over him, anointing him with oil in the name of the Lord. And the prayer of faith will save the sick, and the Lord will raise him up."* Once we anoint someone or something with Anointing Oil then we believe God for a visitation of His Kingdom and Presence.

In prayer we are to take authority over sickness and demonic forces. Jesus cursed the fig tree and it dried up and died. We are to do the same with sicknesses or demonic spirits. We are to have faith and speak to the mountains in our lives. God will anoint us when we step out in faith. Be bold, brave, and have faith in the Power of God. Matthew 21:18-22 says,

> *"Now in the morning, as He returned to the city, He was hungry. And seeing a fig tree by the road, He came to it and found nothing on it but leaves, and said to it, "Let no fruit grow on you ever again." Immediately the fig tree withered away. And when the disciples saw it, they marveled, saying, "How did the fig tree wither away so soon?" So Jesus answered and said to them, "Assuredly, I say to you, if you have faith and do not doubt, you will not only do what was done to the fig tree, but also if you say to this mountain, 'Be removed and be cast into the sea,' it will be done. And whatever things you ask in prayer, believing, you will receive."*

Jesus cursed the fig tree and it responded to His Words and Authority. Jesus used this natural example to show us a spiritual truth. When we speak we are to curse the sickness or enemy. It will dry up and die if you have faith. Jesus said that if you believe you will receive. This has to be prayed according to the Will of God to receive it.

Jesus just showed us that it is the Will of God for us to have faith to take authority over the enemy and his assignments toward us. Luke 10:19 says, *"Behold, I give you the authority to trample on serpents and scorpions, and over all the power of the enemy, and nothing shall by any means hurt you."* Don't ever be afraid to act in faith and look or feel weird. Listen to the Word of God and the Holy Spirit and obey Them and God will do the rest! It is your right as a Child of God to have authority over the enemy. Use your authority and rebuke thoughts, sicknesses, and any attack the enemy sends your way. Be bold and watch the Lord show His Strength and it will build your faith!

The Armor of God

The Bible declares that we are in a battle with a clever enemy. We have a mission, and we need to be equipped to complete that mission. The battle is a spiritual battle, and we have to use spiritual Armor to fight it. The Bible tells us in Ephesians 6:11 to put on the whole Armor of God, "_Put on the whole armor of God, that you may be able to stand against the schemes of the devil._" We cannot just put on a few elements of the Armor and forget the rest. The Armor is designed by God and must be studied carefully for understanding and application purposes. The Armor of God is supernatural, and we need it to fight against the Devil's schemes. He is smart, and He knows how to defeat us when we are not wearing the Armor.

The Armor is explained in Ephesians (NLT) 6:13-18,

"Therefore, put on every piece of God's armor so you will be able to resist the enemy in the time of evil. Then after the battle, you will still be standing firm. Stand your ground, putting on the belt of Truth and the body armor of God's Righteousness. For shoes, put on the peace that comes from the Good News so that you will be fully prepared. In addition to all of these, hold up the shield of faith to stop the fiery arrows of the Devil. Put on salvation as your helmet, and take the sword of the Spirit, which is the Word of God. Pray in the Spirit at all times and on every occasion. Stay alert and be persistent in your prayers for all believers everywhere."

We are to wear the Belt of Truth, which is to believe in the Word of God. We are to use the Truth from the Word of God to stabilize us. A belt is used to hold our pants on tight while keeping our shirt tucked in. This way, we can be active and not worry about our pants falling down, tripping us up. The Truth of God keeps us held together and gives us confidence so we can do what God has called us to do. In Biblical times they wore what would resemble a robe or tunic with a loose belt wrapped about it for most occasions. When they were going to do something physical, they used the belt to tie up their tunic or robes. They called this girding their loins, and usually, it was to fight. It is vital to believe the whole

Word of God, so the Belt of Truth can support you in anything you do for the Lord.

The Breast Plate of Righteousness (Body Armor) is an important part of the Armor. The Breast Plate covers your most vital organs. God's Righteousness covers us when we are submitted to Him and being filled with the Spirit of the Lord. Having a clear conscience protects us from the schemes of the Devil. We are walking upright with our integrity. Most importantly, God's Breastplate protects us from the enemy's attacks supernaturally as well. The Devil has many schemes, and this is why we wear the Armor. The Breastplate causes us to rest in Christ's finished work on the cross and helps us to relax and use this as Armor trusting in the Lord.

The Shoes we wear for the Armor are to be used to spread the Gospel of Peace. We are not to be quick to run to evil but to follow God and be led by His Word as a Lamp unto our feet and a Light to our path (Psalm 119:105). The Roman Soldier had spikes on the bottom of their shoes like a football cleat. This helped them to dig into the ground to get better traction to withstand the enemy. We are to do all of this to stand against the enemy. God wants to equip us so the enemy cannot easily just knock us down. He wants us to stand victoriously balanced and sharing the Good News!

The Helmet of Salvation is used to protect us from the lies of the enemy. We have to keep our minds focused on the benefits of our salvation. We need to make sure to fight the thoughts of the enemy, especially according to salvation. We are to use the Mind of Christ as our mindset. We are to think like Jesus and use the Holy Spirit to guide us in all that we do. God needs to be in our minds, thoughts, and conscience. We are to let Him use our minds to speak to us, guide us, and empower us to do His Will. We should always know that our salvation is secure, and we are protected by Jesus.

The Shield of Faith is an excellent Weapon. We are to have faith in God to protect us from any attack from the enemy. This requires trust in God. All of the Armor is to be used together to have a successful walk with God and to fight and conquer the enemy successfully. The Romans had a shield they used which was almost four feet tall. The shield could be stuck into the ground and knelt behind to protect the warrior. The shield was designed to be linked together with other shields to form a wall of protection. Interestingly enough, the shield was also used to help move wounded soldiers out of the battle. The Shield of Faith helps to quench the arrows or attacks of the enemy. These come in the form of thoughts, as we have learned from previous chapters. They can also be words from other people or demonic attacks. Let's use the Shield of Faith with wisdom, fully trusting, and relying on the Lord to protect us.

The Sword of the Spirit is the Word of God. The Word of God is Powerful and unmatched. The Word gives us wisdom in every situation to outsmart the enemy. The Word gives us strength supernaturally when It is believed or spoken. We can use the Word to speak against the enemy as Jesus did. We are to use the Word to fight. We must memorize It and study It to use It properly. Let us use the Word of God in the most powerful way possible. We are not to only admire how other people use the Sword of the Spirit. We are to personalize It and use It for ourselves. Use the Word of God to defend yourself, attack the enemy, and protect others.

The Armor of God cannot be used without prayer and faith. Prayer is the key to unlocking, putting on, and using the Armor. We are to be always in prayer because the Armor is God's, and It is fueled by faith. We are always to be praying and depending on God to use us and protect us. We are to use the Armor of God because the Devil is not afraid of us if we are not wearing It. The Armor is to be put on, and the Helmet should not allow the enemy to see your face. He should only see the Armor of God and know a Christian is operating It by faith. He will not have a way to penetrate the Armor if It is put on and used correctly. The Armor is a representation of how the Lord and His Word operates to protect us against the enemy. The Armor of God is not made by humans but by the Lord. The Armor is God Himself and His Anointed Powerful Presence. The Bible says to put on Jesus in Romans 13:14, "But put on the Lord Jesus Christ, and make no provision for the flesh, to fulfill its lusts."

Praying in the Spirit

Praying in the Spirit is something that the Lord wants us to do. The Holy Spirit is a Spirit, and there is a heavenly language that the Bible says we don't understand. Paul says that whenever he prays in tongues or in the Spirit, he prays in a language that his mind does not understand, 1 Corinthians 14:14-15 says,

> *"For if I pray in a tongue, my spirit prays, but my understanding is unfruitful. What is the conclusion then? I will pray with the spirit, and I will also pray*

with the understanding. I will sing with the spirit, and I will also sing with the understanding."

However, when we pray in this language, God understands, and we feel energized by the Spirit. Paul says that he will pray in the Spirit and his mind will be unfruitful but he will also pray with understanding which is regular prayer. Paul even says that he will sing in the Spirit and sing with human words. Singing and praying in the Spirit is something we are encouraged to do by the Spirit. It is a powerful and intimate thing and it is an amazing experience.

The Spirit makes intercession for us while our mind is unfruitful or lacking understanding according to Romans 8:26, "Likewise the Spirit also helps in our weaknesses. For we do not know what we should pray for as we ought, but the Spirit Himself makes intercession for us with groanings which cannot be uttered." We feel the Spirit welling up inside of us and wanting to explode. We have to allow the Holy Spirit to come out and make intercession or communicate with the Father. We must let the Holy Spirit Communicate with God the Father who is a Spirit. It is like getting an update on your phone or computer. You must let them re-align so your firewall is updated and active.

You must study the Scriptures to fully understand the supernatural things God wants to do through you. The Gifts of the Spirit (1 Corinthians 12:8-10) are all supernatural, just like the Fruits of the Spirit (Galatians 5:22-23). We cannot fully understand these things with our natural minds, but that does not mean that they are not real and powerful. The enemy doesn't want us to even talk about the supernatural Gifts that the Holy Spirit has for us. However, we should rightly divide the Word of Truth and ask for everything that God wants us to have. Have faith and allow your intelligence, flesh, and religious beliefs to be offended by your lack of understanding or lack of control of the Holy Spirit moving the way He wants to move. Don't put God in a box! If you doubt then you will not receive anything from God. Faith is the Key to receiving in God's Kingdom!

By faith, you believed that Jesus Christ is the Son of God and that you needed forgiveness. The Bible told you this, and that's why you believed It, right? You decided to act by faith, and then you received salvation. This is no different from the Gifts of the Spirit. The Bible says that They are real, and that God wants you to have Them. You must receive Them by faith just as you have accepted Jesus as your Savior. You felt God forgive you of your sins when you prayed. Just ask God to give you the Gifts of the Spirit. When you read the Word, you will understand Them better and can pray to receive Them. You should pray in the Spirit daily until you receive confirmation and peace.

You will not necessarily blurt out in tongues because God will not move on you without your permission. God uses whatever you allow Him to use. If you allow Him to move and to use your mouth to speak in tongues, then He will. He will not do anything unless you allow Him to do it. The Spirit inside of you will overflow out of your belly and be filtered through your mouth. It will be explosive but you control the tempo. Allow God to move and have faith. The Spirit will not force this process. Practice this when you are alone. Allow the Spirit to move through you even if it is just a few syllables at a time. The Spirit will take over your mouth and flow faster and more powerful. This is just like regular prayer. We have to start off with a few words and then God leads us to pray for others, ourselves, and His Will. You are being led by the Spirit whether you pray with words or in the Spirit.

We should desire to have a deeper walk with God and to passionately want the things of the Spirit as 1 Corinthians 14:12 says, "*Even so you since you are zealous for spiritual gifts, let it be for the edification of the church that you seek to excel.*" Using the Gifts of the Spirit takes faith and patience. It is like having a new Smartphone, and you have to figure it out and not just put it in your pocket. You want to explore the phone, see what it is capable of, and use the apps. We must be willing to trust God so He can show us how to use Them. Studying the Word and being mentored by a mature Spirit-Filled Believer is very helpful.

The Bible says we are to fan into flames the Gift of God inside of us. We have to stir up the Gift of God inside of us which is the Holy Spirit by praying in the Spirit according to 2 Timothy 1:6 NLT, "This is why I remind you to fan into flames the spiritual gift God gave you when I laid my hands on you." Fan into flames means to force oxygen to embers on a fire where the fire is not visible. Another version says to stir up the Gift of God inside of us. This is also a reference to stirring the embers until a fire visibly starts. The Spirit is always willing to be ignited to cause us to be on fire for God. We must pray in the Spirit to get the motivation, Power, and encouragement. This will help us to fight our flesh, the enemy, and serve God with Power from the Holy Spirit that dwells within us.

Pleading the Blood of Jesus

Praying is a powerful tool, and something we are supposed to do frequently. The Blood of Jesus is extremely Powerful, just like the Name of Jesus. The Blood of Jesus makes the enemy scared. We must have a firm grasp on why the Blood of Jesus is essential. Mary, the mother of Jesus, was impregnated by the Holy Spirit. The Father supplied the material to impregnate Mary. This made the Baby and the Blood of Jesus extremely Special. We are washed and cleansed by the Blood of Jesus Revelations 1:5 says, "*And from Jesus Christ, the faithful witness, the firstborn from the dead, and the ruler over the kings of the earth. To Him who loved us and washed us from our sins in His own Blood.*" His Blood redeems everyone who asks and has the Power to save.

The Blood of Jesus is the most Powerful and Precious Substance in the Universe. The Power of God resides in the Blood. The Blood of Jesus gives us authority because of what Jesus did on the cross. He shed His Blood seven times on the Earth as the High Priest did in the Old Testament at the Mercy Seat. We access all of God's Benefits when we pray and plead the precious Blood of Jesus. Just say, "Heavenly Father I plead the Blood of Jesus right now over my life, I accept all of the benefits of the Blood of Jesus that was shed for me." God will pour out His Spiritual Blessings upon you when you do this by faith. For a full book on this subject, I recommend "The Power of the Blood" by H. A. Maxwell Whyte. Look up all the Scriptures you can find on the Blood of Jesus and study It's Power as well. God is Amazing!

Casting Out Demons

Casting out demons is part of spiritual warfare as a Christian. As the days grow more evil there will be more manifestations of evil happening. Dealing with someone who is possessed by an evil spirit is not an everyday occurrence. When you are walking in the Spirit and close to God then you have the Anointing of God on your life. The Holy Spirit is on you in a special way and it makes the enemy mad. People who are serving the enemy are walking with demonic spirits. These demonic spirits will use that person to attack you in many different ways. You will be persecuted by them and they will even be unaware sometimes why they are doing it. Anyone can be oppressed by the enemy to the point of possession. If you are a Christian or a non-believer you can listen to the enemy and follow him for a season. If you fully give into sin then you can invite spirits into your life. When you or another person has been doing certain activities they can be oppressed or possessed by a demon.

Oppression is when a demon or multiple demons try to get you to sin and they continually oppress or afflict you. They can oppress you by putting crazy thoughts in your head for days or weeks at a time to try to get you to be depressed or have anxiety for example. This oppression is intensified if you do nothing about it. These demonic spirits will try to dominate you and make you give into temptation or to fear them. Oppression comes in many forms. You can be oppressed by continual temptation and voices that do not stop. I feel like I have had seasons in my life where I was walking around rebuking the enemy all day long. I was so immersed in oppression that I could not feel the Presence of God. The enemy wants to make you think or feel that God is not real or has left you. This causes hopelessness and despair.

The oppression of the enemy will last as long as you allow it to last. It reminds me of bed bugs. My grandmother had them from nurses visiting her house taking care of her. We hired a company and got rid of them within a few days of noticing them. The company came out and cleaned everything. They put mattress covers with zippers on the mattress and box spring to suffocate any remaining bugs or eggs. They removed the bugs by rooting them out and directly spraying them with a poison. They came out a few times after that and found one or two bugs each time until they all were found and killed.

After 1 month they were completely gone. Bed bugs can turn into a nasty infestation and can take over the whole house if left untreated. They torment you in your sleep. They attack you and then hide as if they do not exist. You start to think that it might be something else doing it. It is hard to find them unless you intentionally look for them because you see the signs they are attacking you. They can stay alive for up to a year without having any blood from a host. They can squeeze into places the thickness of a credit card. Demons are the same way. They will stay around if they are fed just a little bit. They have to be removed (Rebuked) or starved out to go away. Poison will kill bed bugs but you must use the Power of God to get rid of demons.

Oppression can be very heavy and terrifying. It is a storm of demonic voices, demonic presence, and demonic activity. Demonic activity can make you feel trapped and immobilized. This can be demonic nightmares, demonic visitation, and overwhelming feelings of evil. You can be oppressed without being in sin and if you submit to them then you can become possessed. You have to rebuke the enemy or you are allowing them to stay. It's like a criminal kicking down your door and you did nothing to stop them from coming into your house and holding you hostage. Evil will prevail if you simply do nothing to stop it.

Possession is simply not rebuking the enemy and allowing them to take control of your temple. Anyone can allow the enemy to come into their lives. It is a sin to give into fear or demonic intimidation. If you allow the enemy to oppress you long enough without doing anything then, "It is easier to just give up." That is the lie the enemy tells you. If you don't fight with the Power of Jesus then the Devil will have a field day with you. You are allowing the demons to come in and take you hostage. Possession is serious and you have to fight against the enemy. You are choosing the Devil if you are not choosing to fight. You don't have to be a superhero in the faith to rebuke demons. It is not hard to do unless you are trying to do it in your strength (Flesh). If you are trying to do it in your strength then it is impossible! Matthew 17:19-20 says,

"Then the disciples came to Jesus privately and said, "Why could we not cast it out?" So Jesus said to them, "Because of your unbelief; for assuredly, I say to you, if you have faith as a mustard seed, you will say to this mountain, 'Move from here to there,' and it will move; and nothing will be impossible for you."

If you fight against them then you will have victory if you repent of your sins and pray with the Power of Jesus for them to leave. You just need faith the size of a mustard seed. That means you have to simply believe that Jesus will show up when you pray to Him and ask Him to deliver you.

You must be confident and have faith when you pray against the enemy. Repent of your sins and call upon the Lord to forgive you of your sins and fill your temple. The Devil will challenge your resolve and will try to see if he can come back and break you down so that you will surrender to him again. Matthew 12:43-45 says,

"When an unclean spirit goes out of a man, he goes through dry places, seeking rest, and finds none. Then he says, 'I will return to my house from which I came.' And when he comes, he finds it empty, swept, and put in order. Then he goes

and takes with him seven other spirits more wicked than himself, and they enter and dwell there; and the last state of that man is worse than the first."

You must continually fight the enemy every time he comes back to test your defenses. If the Lord is set up as your defender then the Devil will have to leave again. If you have not fully surrendered to the Lord then the enemy has a place to come back and stay again. Make sure that you fully repent and start serving the Lord. If you don't then the state of that person will be worse than it was before because the demons will come back with backup.

I have had demons manifest right in front of me and gave me no warning. Have no fear! God gave you a Spirit of Power to deal with demonic spirits. This is all done by the Authority God gave us in Jesus. It is not your special power or good works that allows you to do anything. The Devil is powerful and his kingdom has authority in this World. You need to use the Authority and Power of God to cast out these demonic spirits. Jesus is unmatched in Power. He gave us the Power of God through the Holy Spirit which is stronger than a demon. God's Power is unmatched and It is ours to use according to Mark 16:17-18,

If you are walking with the Lord and demons are attacking you through another person or manifesting through them (Possession) then you have the authority to cast them out. Demons manifest when they are intimidated. Let the Lord guide you but be courageous and firm. Stand your ground and have faith in the Lord. The demon may come out right away after you command it to or it may take awhile. Make sure you are prayed up and that you give it direction when you cast it out. Jesus cast the demons out and sent them into pigs. Make sure that you command them to come out and leave your house and to not come back. Allow the Lord to guide you in this process.

I have had demons manifest right in front of me and gave me no warning. Have no fear! God gave you a Spirit of Power to deal with demonic spirits. This is all done by the Authority God gave us in Jesus. It is not your special power or good works that allows you to do anything. The Devil is powerful and his kingdom has authority in this World. You need to use the Authority and Power of God to cast out these demonic spirits. Jesus is unmatched in Power. He gave us the Power of God through the Holy Spirit which is stronger than a demon. God's Power is unmatched and It is ours to use according to Mark 16:17-18,

"And these signs will follow those who believe: In My name they will cast out demons; they will speak with new tongues; they will take up serpents; and if they drink anything deadly, it will by no means hurt them; they will lay hands on the sick, and they will recover."

Jesus said that believers will cast out demons. It is our job and Jesus has entrusted it to us. The enemy cannot overtake us if we fight against him with true faith.

You must bind the strong man (Demon) when you are casting out demons. The demon has set up shop in the person and you must bind the demon by taking authority over it. When you bind a demonic spirit that causes it to be tied up spiritually. Once you bind the demon you should tell it to shut up and rebuke it out of the person. Matthew 12:28-29 says,

> *"If I cast out demons by the Spirit of God, surely the kingdom of God has come upon you. Or how can one enter a strong man's house and plunder his goods, unless he first binds the strong man? And then he will plunder his house."*

Jesus is saying here that we have to bind (Tie up) the strong man or demon then the Holy Spirit can have full reign of the house if the person accepts Him. So we must address and directly speak to the demon inside a person then take authority over it and cast it out. I typically say, "I bind you demon in Jesus Name and I command you to come out right now!" I will also say, "Shut up demon, I rebuke you in Jesus Name. Come out right now and do not come back." If you can have other people fasting and praying for you while you are both doing this then that is best. Jesus sent them out in pairs so it is best not to cast out demons alone. They absolutely hate it when you plead, sing about, or talk about the Blood of Jesus.

Once the demons come out of the person it is imperative to share the Gospel with them. They need to repent of their sins and accept Jesus as their Savior. Their temple will be invaded again if they do not get filled with the Holy Spirit by being born again. Whoever you have prayed for needs to break the Devil's Contract in their life in whatever area they were allowing the Devil to have access. They need to be mentored and get in Church immediately. They need to dedicate their lives fully to Jesus Christ. The Bible says these demons will come back and try to take over their temple again. This person must be ready or they will just accept the demons back in again because of fear or another reason. The need to learn how to fight against the Devil and his schemes.

The Bible-Believing Church

Practical warfare includes attending a Bible-based Church. When I say a Bible-based Church, I am talking about a Church that submits to the Bible. Some Churches submit themselves to Religion and not to the Bible. If the Bible says that we should sing and play instruments to the Lord, we should do both. The Church of Christ's Religion does not believe this. If the Bible says we should not pray to idols and worship them then we should not do that. It's simple. No excuses or listening to complicated deceitful lies from the enemy! The Catholic Religion does this practice. If the Bible says that we should anoint with oil and pray for healing then we should be doing this (James 5:14). Most Non-Denominational Churches believe in doing this. A good Bible-based Church will have the Gifts of the Spirit active in more than just one believer in the Church. The Pastor can give a Word of Knowledge or Prophecy at a Church. However, some Pastors do not allow anybody else to operate in the Gifts of the Spirit. This is not correct as we see in 1 Corinthians 12:4-11,

> *"There are diversities of gifts, but the same Spirit. There are differences of ministries, but the same Lord. And there are diversities of activities, but it is the same God who works all in all. But the manifestation of the Spirit is given to each one for the profit of all: for to one is given the word of wisdom through the Spirit, to another the word of knowledge through the same Spirit, to another faith by the same Spirit, to another gifts of healings by the same Spirit, to another the working of miracles to another prophecy, to another discerning of spirits, to another different kinds of tongues, But one and the same Spirit works all these things, distributing to each one individually as He wills."*

We are the Body of Christ, so God has given the Body many Gifts, and they are dispersed throughout the Body as He wants, and it is not up to the Pastor. Anybody can start a Church and declare himself or herself as the Pastor. This does not mean that they have the ultimate Authority of God. This does not mean that they are perfect and that they are the only person that hears from God. However, since you are going to that Church, then the Pastor is your spiritual authority, and you should submit to him. If you see or think he is doing something that isn't Biblical, then you should pray and ask God to reveal it to the Pastor. If you feel that the Pastor or something in the Church is not right then, it is probably best to move on to a Church where the Holy Spirit is not being held captive from moving the way He wants.

When you go to a Bible-based Church, you should see the Father, the Son, and the Holy Spirit being worshiped and working. The Holy Spirit should be evident throughout the service. Worship should be Spirit-filled, and you should be able to feel the Presence of God during Worship. The Pastor should be preaching the Word of God accurately and there should be an anointing on the message that you hear. The Pastor or Elders should give new people an altar call to get saved and minister to the existing members through the Laying on of Hands (1 Timothy 4:14) and the Gifts of the Spirit. When you come to Church, you should be challenged to get closer to the Lord. You should feel the Lord in worship, calling you to get closer. You should feel the Lord preaching to you, challenging you to repent and get closer to Him. In addition, you should feel the challenge of using your faith in prayer to get closer to the Lord during the altar call or time of ministry. The Biblical Doctrine of the Laying on of Hands should be occurring during each service. The Holy Spirit should be able to do what He wants to do with deliverance from the enemy and the equipping of the Saints for Ministry (Ephesians 4:12).

You can go to a Church with acceptable worship, but the preaching isn't that good, and there is no altar call. You can go to a Church that has ok worship excellent preaching and no altar call. You can go to a Church with ok worship, ok preaching, and then a powerful ministry time at the altar call. You can see people being healed and demons being cast out. Each one of these three examples are not perfect. They limit the Lord, and I don't believe it is best to attend one of these Churches. Satan will try to trap you into thinking that you should go there and change the way that Church operates and be a hero, but I believe it is best for you to go to a Church operating in all three of these consistently. You shouldn't stay and try to fight the system because the head Pastor has his mind made up. There is a spirit of Religion operating in that Church and the Pastor will not repent quickly, especially by the word of just an ordinary person who's attending the Church. It is best to move on.

God will give you wisdom on where to go to Church. However, you should always be looking for a Church that is genuinely worshiping God, preaching God, and showing God's Power. I have attended many Churches, where the Pastor will preach a powerful sermon on healing. It will make you want to get out of your seat and go down front to get prayed for and healed. Suddenly the Pastor will cut the sermon short just in time for everyone to be dismissed for football Sunday. He just will wave goodbye to everybody and disappear behind the curtain. There is no time for the Holy Spirit to confirm the message that the Pastor was preaching. It should be a crime not to have intimate worship, profound preaching, and powerful ministry at the end.

Don't sell yourself short and miss out on the full Plan of God for a Church service. He wants the Church service to be a fantastic time with Him to change your life every Sunday, not just when a guest speaker comes or when you visit another Church. Seek after God, experience Him, and don't get comfortable. If you get comfortable, then the enemy and your flesh are happy! As with every good Church service, there should be a time of prayer and ministry at the end. Therefore, it is time to pray. If you haven't received Power and the Holy Spirit's Baptism, then now is a chance to go deeper with the Lord and receive what he has for you. God will use you as a mighty weapon against the enemy, but we need to have supernatural Power to fight this battle.

Let's ask God to fill us more with His Spirit and to illuminate His Power in our lives. Repeat this prayer, "Heavenly Father, I come to You now, by faith, I want more of You, I need more of You, help me Lord to fight this fight of faith. By faith, I ask You for the Baptism of the Holy Spirit; please fill me with Your Spirit. I receive Your Power from on high. I pray in faith for the Gifts of the Spirit Lord; I ask Lord that You would give me the Wisdom to fight against the enemy. Help me use the Gifts of the Spirit to edify the Church. Help me to set other people free. Fill me with Your Spirit and everything You want me to have. I trust You Lord. Please fill me with the Waters that run deep from the well within your Spirit. Lord, I want more of You, help me to serve You. Help me to fight my flesh, and to do Your Will, in Jesus Name I pray. Amen!"

Allow the Holy Spirit to pray through you in the Spirit right now. This will be a new experience for you but allow the Holy Spirit to gently guide you in praying in tongues. Be patient and have faith. Jesus said out of your belly with flow Rivers of Living Water. The Holy Spirit will start to fill your temple, belly, or chest area with an overflowing feeling. Allow Him to use your mouth to pray. This will be in utterances that you do not understand. Just practice with a few syllables until the Lord takes over by the Spirit. Don't get frustrated. Practice now. Get your breakthrough. Rebuke doubt and believe while acting in faith. Move your mouth! It may seem weird, and the enemy will tell you that you are wasting your time, but he is lying.

CHAPTER 14

An Unstoppable Royal Priesthood

"But you are a chosen generation, a royal priesthood, a holy nation, His own special people, that you may proclaim the praises of Him who called you out of darkness into His marvelous light." 1 Peter 2:9

Walking closely with God is incomparable to anything this World has to offer. As Christians, we have an unlimited reserve of Power that God wants us to tap into and use. Every time we tap into this Power, we can choose to receive the Fruits or the Gifts of the Spirit. I believe that all Christians are unstoppable when they decide to walk with God. We are called Believers. So why is that important? It is an honor to be called a Believer. A Believer is not just a person that believes in Jesus Christ. A Believer is someone who believes everything the Bible has to say. So, let me ask you a question, are you a Believer?

Now, if you said yes to that, then that is awesome. However, you have to understand the question that I'm asking. The Bible says some things that the culture does not agree with at all. If you're a friend with the World, then you want to please the culture. You have to choose to go against the culture and the people involved and identifying with the culture. The Bible says that this culture is evil. Therefore, if the Bible says something, we must believe It is the Word of God. It is not to be read with a skeptical mindset. We are not supposed to read the Bible and just take out what we want to apply to our lives and leave the rest. The Bible is referred to as the Whole Counsel of God. We must understand, believe, and apply all of It to our lives.

As a true Believer, you are never to doubt the Word of God. If God says that you can be healed, then there is no disputing that. If you pray and don't get healed right away, you need to pray and ask God to understand why you didn't get healed. The Bible has plenty of situations where healing has taken place. We have to believe the Word of God and get rid of our expectations or mindless interpretations. The Lord heals numerous different ways. If you have a major medical problem and God told you exactly how to get cured without going to the doctor and spending thousands of dollars, would you do it? Would you get angry or mad at God for what He told you to do? It seems ridiculous but there is an example in the Bible about how somebody treated the Lord whenever he gave them instructions on how to be healed. 2 Kings 5:10-11 says,

> *"Then Elisha sent him a messenger, who said, "Go and wash yourself seven times in the Jordan, and your flesh will be restored, and you will be clean." But Naaman went away angry, saying, "I thought that he would surely come out, stand and call on the name of the Lord his God, and wave his hand over the spot to cure my leprosy."*

Therefore, you see here, the Lord gave someone the answer to their prayer and told them how to get healed. However, this guy got mad and left because his expectations were not met. God is not concerned with meeting your expectations. God is concerned with you being humble and following His Word. It does not matter how absurd or counterculture His Word is. God wants us to follow Him and have faith; this is the only way that we are going to please God (Hebrews 11:6).

The Devil likes to use his Contract to destroy our faith. When we have Faith but accept the Contract of Doubt then it cancels our faith. We are suppose to pray and believe without doubt Matthew 21:21 says,

> *"So Jesus answered and said to them, "Assuredly, I say to you, if you have faith and do not doubt, you will not only do what was done to the fig tree, but also if you say to this mountain, 'Be removed and be cast into the sea,' it will be done. And whatever things you ask in prayer, believing, you will receive."*

If you hear the Scripture and have a Contract of Deception then it cancels out your freedom. If you have a Contract of Doubt and a Contract of Deception then it cancels out any change in your life. If you hear the Word of God and have a Contract of Doubt (Not trusting God or the Word) then it cancels out any possibility of a fruitful crop. The seed is rejected by the soil and you will not reap a harvest. We have to FULLY believe and FULLY trust God and His Word or nothing will happen because we are double-minded.

God wants us to believe Him at His Word. Healing is only one thing in the Bible that requires faith. As we spoke about in the second chapter, God's Word is the Absolute Truth. It doesn't matter how you feel about It, what other people say about It, or what the enemy says about It. God wants us to have faith in His Word without any doubt. If we have faith and we doubt His Word a little bit, then that cancels out faith. If we believe God can heal us because He has healed people in the Bible before, but don't believe that He will heal us, then nothing will happen. The Bible says a double-minded man is unstable in all of his ways. Jesus said to have faith without doubting (Matthew 21:21).

If you believe the Scriptures, then miracles will happen in your life. You will see people get healed; you will see demons being cast out, see people being saved, and see miraculous things if you only believe. An unbeliever can go to a Church and see all these things happen, and they don't have to have any faith because they're just spectators. You will see all these things happen and be involved in them if you have faith. God will use you to bring His Kingdom into this culture. God wants His Kingdom to reign in this World despite the culture. The Kingdom is a system that has an order to It that destroys chaos and doubt. The Kingdom of God has a hierarchy, and what God says is true.

Unbelief will cripple your faith. Mark 16:14 says, "*Later He appeared to the eleven as they sat at the table; and He rebuked their unbelief and hardness of heart, because they did not believe those who had seen Him after He had risen.*" Jesus rebuked them for not believing. He was with them every day, did miracles in their sight, taught, and trained them daily. Jesus rebuked them for their hardness of heart. They allowed the culture and the enemy to cause them not to believe. Other people came and proclaimed that Jesus had risen, but they shrugged it off. They did not believe, and their hearts were hardened. This is what doubt will do to you. It will turn into unbelief, and your heart will be hardened. You will no longer be able to see or believe the things of God. Just like many people today do not believe in healing or other supernatural things in the Bible. God can use any Christian today. You do not have to be perfect to be used by God. You only have to believe. These signs will follow them that believe, Mark 16:15-18 says,

"And He said to them, "Go into all the world and preach the Gospel to every creature. He who believes and is baptized will be saved, but he who does not believe will be condemned. And these signs will follow those who believe: In My Name, they will cast out demons; they will speak with new tongues; they will take up serpents; and if they drink anything deadly, it will by no means hurt them; they will lay hands on the sick, and they will recover."

God has your back. If you trust in Him, then He will show up! Dare to put God's Word into faith and action. God wants you to believe. Jesus said that if you have the faith of a mustard seed, you will say to this mountain be uprooted and cast into the sea. For us in the natural realm to think of a mountain being uprooted and thrown into the sea is impossible. This same logic can be applied to casting out demons or healing the sick. It's impossible without God. Have faith in God, Matthew 19:26 says, *"But Jesus looked at them and said to them, "With men, this is impossible, but with God, all things are possible."* Jesus is looking at you today and telling you that with God, all things are possible if you only believe.

God is calling you to a life of faith and trust in Him. Your friends and family may not answer God's Call, but He wants you to answer the Call. He wants us to believe the Bible and do what It says. We are to lay hands on the sick and pray for them. The Bible says that when we pray for the sick and lay our hands on them, they will recover. This is the Biblical Christian Doctrine of the Laying on of Hands. Have faith and trust God for the miraculous. Peter got out of the boat when the Lord asked him. He didn't ask the other people in the boat because they weren't ready to even take that first step out of the boat. With all of this training, you are ready to trust in the Lord and take Him at His Word! Timothy received from the Lord by having hands laid on Him in 1 Timothy 4:14, *"Do not neglect the gift that is in you, which was given to you by prophecy with the laying on of the hands of the eldership."* Laying your hands on someone and praying for them can transfer a spiritual Anointing or Gifts to that person. Be led by the Holy Spirit and pray by faith.

Ministry is our calling here on Earth. Many people think that ministry is only preaching at a Church. The Bible says that we are all called to preach, and we are to be ready in season and out of season. The Great Commission is a calling for all people to go and preach the Gospel. It's not only to preach the Gospel but also to pray for the sick and show God's Power. The Devil is showing his power in the World today through witchcraft and other satanic things. God wants to show the World His Power too. He loves everybody, and He wants to get their attention. When God showed His Power to cast out demons in Acts, all of the witches burned their books, repented, and got saved.

Ministry is important, and God wants us to minister to the people around us. He may be calling you to another country or to another place besides where you live right now. However, right now, God has you where you're at, and the people around you need to hear the Gospel. The Gospel is Good News, so you shouldn't have a problem sharing good news, right? We don't have a problem giving a useful review on Yelp or telling other people about our experiences at the restaurant that we visited, right? You should not be ashamed to share the Gospel and tell others what Jesus has done for you.

If you're in love with somebody, then you can't shut up about them. When you get around someone who just met somebody, they are so excited to tell you about them. They get to the point where there almost annoying with all of the details and have plenty of stories. However, if you just watch their face, they will smile, and their eyes are going to light up because they are exhilarated with their relationship. If you have had a life-changing experience with Jesus at any point in your life, you would be excited about it. Sin and this world crept in at some point and tried to throw water on your fire. It is up to us to daily fan that fire into flames and let it consume us again, 2 Timothy 1:6 says, "*Therefore I remind you to stir up the gift of God which is in you through the laying on of my hands.*" We have to choose daily to crucify this flesh and follow God.

Suppose we have given into the flesh for a prolonged period and believe that it will take a little bit of time to get back to a close relationship with God. God forgives you instantly when you ask Him, but we have to crucify our flesh, and this does not feel exhilarating. Just like going to the gym and working out for the first time in years, it is going to leave you sore and not wanting to do much. When we crucify our flesh, it's going to cry out, scream, and not want to obey. However, Paul says he brings his body into subjection to obey God in 1 Corinthians 9:27, "*But I discipline my body and bring it into subjection, lest, when I have preached to others, I myself should become disqualified.*" This is not through works, but this is through crucifying his flesh to get closer to God. You can't give your flesh anything that it asks for because all it wants to do is overindulge on evil desires and distract you from your relationship with God.

Choosing to minister to others is Biblical and mandated by God. When we minister to others, we are fulfilling our call from God. Our purpose in this life is to be used by God and shine His Light in the darkness. When God moves through us, the Fruits of the Spirit and the Joy of the Lord are abundant. It is an absolute pleasure and joy to be used by God. I have been in the middle of praying for someone and just broke out laughing in the Spirit because I was overjoyed by the Spirit of God moving on me. The other person broke out laughing too, and we forgot what we were praying about but didn't care.

God wants to flood us with His Spirit to the point of overflowing. Don't put God in a box. God can do whatever He wants despite what you think or how you feel about it. Being critical is the result of a religious spirit trying to pop back up. Have faith and believe God. Test the spirits (1 John 4:1), but if it is God then submit to what He is doing at that time in your life. He will bring you Peace and show you what it is He is trying to do, just don't grieve the Holy Spirit based on your past experiences. We can get scared of change or fear something our Church growing up didn't teach. Don't be afraid of God. God is gentle and will lead you to the Truth. Imagine growing up in the Islamic faith, and you have to change everything you have learned. Don't be afraid. Don't limit God! If you hear voices telling you to limit God, then rebuke it!

I know that we spoke about worship before, but something extraordinary happened since I wrote about it last. In the story of Mary and Martha, Mary was busy trying to do things to prepare for the arrival of Jesus. Mary dropped everything when the Lord showed up and sat at His Feet and worshiped Him intimately. Ministry can keep us busy, and ministry is a great thing, but we have to spend time with the Lord before ministering to do it effectively. I was in worship earlier, and after a few songs, I was tempted to end that time in worship because I needed to get up and finish this last chapter of the book. The thought came in my mind, and I ignored it. I put on another song and worshiped longer. After worship was over, I sat in the Lord's Presence and just listened for a while. I heard the Lord say to me that I have chosen rightly! My heart melted like butter. I realized that the Lord was telling me that he was pleased with me for choosing to worship Him instead of giving up and finishing this last chapter. I had not reached the Holy of Holies in the Presence of God in an intimate way. If I stopped worshiping, I would have been compromising.

I chose to spend time with Him instead of working for Him. There is a big difference. One is filling and brings Joy and Contentment, and the other drains that out of you. Now don't get me wrong, ministry can also fill you with Joy, but it does get depleted through serving and ministering. I encourage you to minister to others but never do it unless you are filled to the brim and overflowing with the Presence of God. I went into the prayer room many years ago at the place I was preaching and got down on my face and laid down in my suit and put my face on the ground. I started praying to the Lord because I wanted Him to fill me and be the one that was ministering instead of me in my strength. I remember the Lord saying to me, "That this (On my face) is where I want you." When we are in prayer and entirely relying on God, then He powerfully uses us. We are genuinely surrendering and crucifying the flesh and wanting His Will to be done in our lives. There is no other way to minister!

When we are talking to other people, we should make sure that we hear from the Lord. I remember going door to door evangelizing and meeting a Chinese man. The door opened, and I asked him if he had any canned goods for our Church. He said he didn't have any, and I asked him if he went to Church anywhere. He said that he goes to a Christian Church and a Buddhist Temple, so he is covered. The Lord spoke to me, and I told the man that even Buddha would say to you to get on one path and stay on it. The man got mad and said, how am I supposed to serve Jesus if I do not know him? I put down my Bible and asked him to join hands with me. I told him I could take him to Jesus right now and asked him to pray with me. I led him in the Sinner's Prayer, and he was born again. He started crying, and he was full of Joy.

Since I listened to the Lord, within 30 seconds of me knocking on the door, that man was saved from going to hell. Doing ministry without being filled by the Spirit or led by the Spirit is exhausting. If I had not listened to what the Lord was telling me to say, then I could have talked to him for eight hours before he decided for Christ, or maybe he never would have even made that decision. However, the Lord gave me a Word of Wisdom, and It cut straight through his heart, thoughts, emotions, and excuses. The man was ready to meet Jesus, but he had to get past all of his obstacles first. That one Word of Wisdom destroyed all those barriers. I simply escorted him to meet Jesus.

Ministry can be exhausting, and just like Martha, it can make you start complaining. Martha could not stand it that Mary was sitting there worshiping while she was doing all the work. Luke 10:38-42 says,

"Now it happened as they went that He entered a certain village, and a certain woman named Martha welcomed Him into her house. And she had a sister called Mary, who also sat at Jesus' feet and heard His Word. But Martha was distracted with much serving, and she approached Him and said, "Lord, do You not care that my sister has left me to serve alone? Therefore, tell her to help me." And Jesus answered and said to her, "Martha, Martha, you are worried and troubled about many things. But one thing is needed, and Mary has chosen that good part, which will not be taken away from her."

Jesus is telling us the same thing today. If we don't choose to spend time with the Lord but stay busy working to please Him, then we are missing it. Martha even commands Jesus to tell her to help. Wow. Being in the flesh is ugly, and it does not understand the things of God. Jesus had to explain to her that He considered what she was doing was not the most important. Jesus also had a Word of Knowledge and told her she is worried and troubled about many things. We think we know the Will of God, but we don't in the flesh without the Spirit telling us. Peter tried to build three temples once he saw Jesus, Moses, and Elijah. Peter cut the ear off a person thinking it was God's Will. God will give you discernment and show you how to know Him if you are humble.

What is bothering you today? What is keeping you out of the Presence of God by declaring you worship it instead? Even good things are not a good enough excuse not to be at Jesus' Feet in worship. If you are going to choose Jesus, then He will use you in a mighty way. If you don't choose Jesus as your daily priority, then you will be overwhelmed with sin and not have the Fruits of the Spirit active in your life. Love should always be flowing to us from God and out of us toward others. This means we are in constant communication with God and being filled with His Spirit. If you are showing signs of Martha, then drop everything you are doing and run to Jesus. Stop hurting people and go to Jesus. Just stop, drop, and kneel because the Devil has lit you on fire, and God needs to put it out.

Being under authority is extremely important in the Kingdom of God. God wants us to be involved in a Church. The Pastor is the head of that Church. The Pastor can help you with the spiritual problems that you are dealing with daily. It is crucial to have a spiritual covering that way, and they can direct and mentor you spiritually. When you are involved in a Church, you can be disciplined and taught the things of God. God will use your authority to protect you. There is a special Anointing that God gives people that are under spiritual authority. When you are under authority and obeying that authority, God is pleased with you. You are showing the Lord that you are humble and teachable. You may not agree with everything your leader says, but you should still submit to your authority. Pray for your authority if you have any kind of concerns for them.

The Bible says that we are to pray for one another and confess our sins to one another. It is good to have a prayer partner or someone that you can be real with all the time. This is someone that you can trust to be confidential. When you are in a Church, God can teach you what He wants to show you about the system He set up. God designed the Church to operate according to His Will. The Offices of the Church include Pastors, Evangelists, Apostles, Teachers, and Prophets. You may fall into one of these Offices within the Church, or you may not. That's ok. We are all to preach and teach others and evangelize the lost. It doesn't matter if that is one of the Offices in the Church that you will ever officially have. There are many Gifts of the Spirit to operate within the Church as well. The Church should be serving and resembling the Kingdom of God. The Power of God should be moving in prayer and the Gifts of the Spirit. Not all the Gifts of the Spirit are used in one service or all the time. People use the Gifts of the Spirit by faith. Some people don't have much faith and only use one Gift. The Apostle Paul tells us that we should be craving and coveting the best Gifts.

You shouldn't just get up and walk out of a Church because you do not see all of the Spirit's Gift's moving in the same service. Be patient and let the Holy Spirit lead you. Being in a Church Body full of Spirit-filled Believers where the Holy Spirit is moving is a blessing. There are not many Churches these days that practice all of what the Bible teaches. Get involved in the Church and help and be humble. Stay under authority. God does not want lone rangers. The Devil wants you to think that you're the only one that's right and that you should go off on your own and don't need anybody else. He will isolate you, and then he will slowly cause you to compromise and fall into sin. The Bible says a three-cord strand is not easily broken. He has given us each other as the Body of Christ. Be teachable and be humble. God resists the proud.

Sanctification is a marathon and not a sprint. When we get saved, our spirit is born again. Our flesh is still in the same condition as it was before we got saved. Our flesh is evil and wants us to sin as much as possible. The flesh will continuously war against the Spirit. If you let the flesh take over momentarily, then you will sin. If you stay full of the Spirit and resist your flesh and the Devil, you will not sin (James 4:7). Don't get down on yourself because you are still sinning in certain areas of your life. Walking with God is a choice, and how close you are to God is a choice.

If you're tired of being in sin and want to walk with God, you will walk close to God and resist evil. If you are still struggling with sin because you still want to do it, you will not have a real close relationship with God. This is because you want to leave room for your sin between you and God. Sometimes you can be walking close to God and still give into sin because you have trained yourself to listen to your flesh's voice. Don't give up. Keep fighting. Jesus will help you. Sin will not have dominion over you 1 Corinthians 10:13 says,

> *"No temptation has overtaken you except what is common to mankind. And God is faithful; he will not let you be tempted beyond what you can bear. But when you are tempted, he will also provide a way out so that you can endure it."*

You can win over sin through the Holy Spirit's Power no matter what the Devil tells you. Don't sign a Contract and give up. Break the Contract and serve God. The Devil is a liar!

As you serve Jesus, then you will have a heart for people. People are the mission. Saving them from burning in hell is the ultimate mission in the Great Commission. We also are to be making disciples and walking in faith. If you want to serve God, then you have the Great Commission to follow. Matthew records the Great Commission from Jesus in Matthew 28:18-20,

> *"And Jesus came and spoke to them, saying, All authority has been given to Me in heaven and on earth. Go therefore and make disciples of all the nations, baptizing them in the name of the Father and of the Son and of the Holy Spirit, teaching them to observe all things that I have commanded you; and lo, I am with you always, even to the end of the age. Amen."*

Jesus said all Authority had been given to Him, and He is with us always even till the end of the age. This means all Christians until the end of the World. We are to take His Power and fight evil. We are to preach the Gospel and make disciples. We are to obey all that Jesus taught. Jesus promised the Holy Spirit would come and give them Power. When the Holy Spirit came, Peter explained Biblically why and how this happened (Acts 2:14-47). The Holy Spirit is Real and Powerful. Jesus gave the Holy Spirit to seal us with Power.

God wants to give you the Power to live an overcoming Christian life. The Power of the Holy Spirit is unlocked whenever we believe and trust God for it. I believe the Baptism in the Holy Spirit is a one-time thing. I believe God gives this to you when you are ready to receive it. Once you have reached a place in God where you are surrendered and prepared to move to the next level with Him, you can start believing God for the Holy Spirit's Baptism. The Baptism of the Holy Spirit was given to the Believers who followed Jesus and waited by faith to receive it in the Upper Room. When you reach a place in your life where your ready to serve God and be powerfully used by Him, you will need the Holy Spirit's Baptism. God has already given you Authority over the enemy, and that's why you can rebuke him in your thoughts and life. However, the Power that the Holy Spirit gives you unlocks every spiritual Gift and the Anointing for Ministry.

God wants you to believe the Scriptures and have faith for miracles. Paul said he didn't come with big words but in demonstration and power of the Holy Ghost 1 Corinthians 2:4-5,

"And my speech and my preaching were not with persuasive words of human wisdom, but in demonstration of the Spirit and of power, that your faith should not be in the wisdom of men but in the power of God."

There comes a time where the rubber meets the road. You don't build a car and keep it in the garage. You take it out and show the power that it has on the streets. Do not be afraid to act out in faith, and nothing happen. I have prayed in faith many times, and nothing has happened, I thought. I have followed up with a few people and found that they were not ready, or didn't believe, or just got prayed for because their friend wanted them to.

You never know what is going on, so ask questions before and after if you feel led. They may have made a Contract with the Devil and can't receive from God. It's not your fault if nothing seems to happen when you pray. Pray regardless! Have faith and believe His Word, and He will show up. Study the Scriptures and follow them. The Holy Spirit will give you direction and wisdom! It's ok that people laugh at you and make fun of you. They did it to

Jesus, so they are going to do it to you, too. Not everyone will like you because of the enemy. Some Christians may make fun of you for a season; just pray for them and forgive them quickly. They don't know what spirit they are of when they are doing this.

You are unstoppable if you are following God. You are a Royal Priesthood. God has called us to be a Priest, and we have the Spirit of God that lives directly inside of us. We are of the Royal Lineage of Jesus Christ. Therefore, I believe that we are an Unstoppable Royal Priesthood. When we are following God and believing His Word, then we are unstoppable. Just like in the Book of Job, the Devil had to beg God only to have a little bit of permission to mess with Job's life. God so blesses us that the Devil doesn't have power over us. If we use the Armor of God and walk closely with God, the enemy can't stop us. The Bible says that no weapon formed against us will prosper! We are Christians in the Armor of God, filled with the Spirit of God, growing in the Fruits of the Spirit, while using the Gifts of the Spirit. This is an unstoppable combination and the recipe for Victory!

Now the plans of the enemy may prevent us or delay us but never stop us. We must be Spirit-led in everything that we do. Sometimes when we are prevented from doing something, it may be the Hand of the Lord. Everybody has a specific assignment to complete, while here on this Earth. No two people are alike. I can't reach the people in your life that you can reach. Only you can reach those people. They won't go to Church, so you are the closest thing they have to Church in their life. We all have the same calling in Christ Jesus. People are the mission. Seek first the Kingdom of God, and all these things will be added unto you (Matthew 6:33).

Through everything you have learned from this book, you are on your way to being an extremely sharp weapon against the enemy. The Lord is going to use you mightily to fight the good fight of faith. You have to make sure that you are free to get close to God. You have to make sure that you have broken all of the areas of the Contract you have with the Devil. This will break the cycle of evil in your life. The enemy wants you to be trapped in sin and scared to be close to God. There are unknown gods that people worship. In the Bible, Paul talks about a people group he ran across that had a statue dedicated to an Unknown God (Acts 17:23). In your life, you may have unknown gods that we didn't talk about in this book or that you haven't thought about recently. Pray and ask God to show you what unknown God you are serving. Remember, an idol is anything that you put in between you and God. So, when you're going to pray, or you're going to worship, you may be thinking about this idol during this time. You are thinking about it because it wants to distract you from spending time with God. You have to break the Contract you have made with the enemy.

Only the Power of God can break the Contract that you have made with the enemy. Use this book and the examples in it as a guide to being free. Remember, "If we don't allow God to use us, then we will use something else!" Stay filled with the Spirit so you don't make any contracts. Be on the lookout for the enemy trying to sneak in and make you a prisoner with his lies. Come back as often as you need to so you can read the chapters and fill out the forms in the back of the book because the Devil has the same tactics, and he wants to keep you bound. Show this book to others and make copies of the list to fill out and give to others. Make disciples and help other people to get free from the Devil's Contract. God will bless you and provide you with wisdom on how to do it. This will guide you, but the Holy Spirit will give you the understanding that you need.

Let's pray and ask for the Lord's help in our lives. "Heavenly Father, I come to You right now and humbly ask for Your Favor. Lord help me to serve You. Allow me to follow hard after You. Lord, I surrender my life to You right now, and I ask for You to use me. I give You every idol in my life. I Break the Devil's Contract that I signed with the enemy. I don't want any more idols in my life. Help me, Lord, to serve You, and not anything else. Help me, Lord, to be like You. Help me to minister to others so You can set them free. Let my light so shine before men, that they glorify You, Jesus. Lord, I agree to believe Your Word, no matter what. I have faith in your Word, no matter how I feel. Help me to serve You and not myself. Lord guide me in everything that I do so that nothing can hinder me. No weapon formed against me will prosper! Lord use me in a mighty way so Your Kingdom can come to this Earth with Power. Thank You for making me an Unstoppable Royal Priesthood, I love You, in Jesus Name I pray, Amen!

Saints go with God, remember that you are in Unstoppable Royal Priesthood. No weapon formed against you shall prosper! God is going to use you in a mighty way. Study His Word and stay sharp. Pray every day and surrender to God continually. Find good friends in the Lord and help one another. Get in a good Bible-Believing Church and become a disciple. Disciple others and help them to serve the Lord. Break the Contract in your life that you made with the Devil and help others break the Contract they have made with the Devil as well. God will give you strength as you trust in Him. Fulfill the Great Commission and take Authority over the enemy! May God Bless you and empower you to do His Will, In Jesus Name!

<u>Pastoral Blessing</u>

Receive the Blessing of the Lord,

"God will not allow your foot to be moved; He who keeps you will not slumber. Behold the Lord is your Keeper; the Lord is your shade at your right hand. The Sun shall not strike you by day, nor the moon by night. The Lord shall preserve you from all evil; He shall preserve your soul. The Lord shall preserve your going out and your coming in from this time forth, and even forevermore. The Lord Bless you and Keep you; The Lord make His Face shine upon you, and be gracious to you; The Lord lift up His countenance upon you, And give you Peace!"

Follow us at www.breakingthedevilscontract.org

GLOSSARY

The Word of God- The Bible is the Word of God and was written by the Spirit of God through many different authors. It is the inspired Words of God in written form.

Deliverance- The process of removing any trace of the Devil from a human being including casting out demons and removing demonic strongholds or false teachings.

Church- A building that houses people that believe a certain religion.

Doctrine- A religious belief that becomes part of the foundation of a Church. These beliefs are made into teachings or doctrines. This becomes the core truth of the religion or Church.

Religion- A man-made organization ruled by doctrinal beliefs.

Demonic Strongholds- A place that the enemy occupies in a person that was formed through agreeing with demonic thoughts or the Devil's Contract.

Spirit of Fear- A demonic spirit that tries to infuse fear into humans through thoughts and possession while creating a demonic stronghold.

Spirit of Pride- A demonic spirit that tries to infuse pride into humans through thoughts and possession while creating a demonic stronghold.

Spirits of Lust and Perversion- Demonic Spirits that try to pervert Believers into thinking about and acting out sinful sexual desires.

Spirit of Wrath- A demonic spirit that tries to infuse hate into humans through thoughts and possession while creating a demonic stronghold.

Christian Religion- A religion that is formed from doctrine out of the Christian Bible. Not all Christian Religions have correct Biblical Doctrinal Beliefs.

True Christian- A Believer in Jesus Christ that has invited the Lord Jesus to come into their heart. This Believer has asked for forgiveness of their sins and felt the Lord forgive them. They believe the whole Bible as the Word of God and are born again.

True Christian Church- True Christian Church or "The Church" is made up of True Christians who are indwelt with the Spirit of God with a mission from God found in the

Word of God. The TCC will follow all Biblical mandates for how a Church is to operate in the New Testament.

The Flesh- The Flesh or sin nature is a sinful mindset. This includes the evil desires of your heart. Everyone inherits this sin nature and its desires must be crucified daily and your mind is to be transformed by reading of the Word of God.

Crucify the Flesh- A Biblical practice of denying the evil desires of the flesh in order to obey the Word of God. This can only be successfully accomplished by the Power of the Holy Spirit and submitting to God.

Sanctification- The process of obeying the Word of God and causing your flesh to line up with the Will of God. This is done through submitting to God and allowing His Holy Power of the Holy Spirit to accomplish this task. Our own fleshly efforts can't sanctify us alone. The Holy Spirit gives us power over sin and we can't brag about our flesh accomplishing the task. This involves crucifying the flesh.

Justification- The salvation that occurs from believing and receiving Jesus as your Lord and Savior. The believer becomes Justified or forgiven in the sight of God and welcomed into heaven upon death. This is the new birth the Bible talks about.

The Enemy- This is any evil force that is working against the Will of God. This includes the Devil, demons, and the will of people that are being used by that force.

The Kingdom of Darkness- This is the strategic formation of the enemy that is in direct opposition to the Kingdom of God.

The Devil- The Devil or Lucifer is referred to as the god of this World. He was created by God as an Angel. He was kicked out of Heaven for rebellion against God. He is a created being and is subject to the Power of God and the Name of Jesus.

The Devil's Contract- An agreement made between the enemy and a human. This agreement is an acceptance of demonic doctrine which leads to making that human a slave to the will of the enemy.

The Gospel- This is the message of Jesus Christ (The Good News) and His Sacrificial Death on the cross that allows anyone to be forgiven of their sins that believes and receives Him as their Savior. The Gospel includes the prophecies concerning Him, His Birth, Sinless Life, Sacrificial Death on the cross, and Resurrection. The Gospel includes every aspect of Jesus. The whole message of Jesus should be shared to all non-believers for the Great Commission and salvation for all who will believe (John 3:16).

The Sinner's Prayer- A prayer that allows a person to repent of their sins, believe in Jesus as their Savior, and accept Him as Lord. This prayer is said by a person confirming their belief in the Gospel, repentance of a sinful lifestyle, and is the accepting of Jesus as their Savior. If a person prays this prayer with sincerity, then the person praying it will be saved. They will feel the Lord forgiving them and coming into their heart causing them to be born again.

Example Sinner's Prayer

"Heavenly Father I believe that Jesus is Your Son. I believe that He was born of a virgin and came to the Earth as was prophesied in the Old Testament. I believe that He lived a sinless life and was persecuted on the Earth. I believe that He healed the sick and was God manifested in human form. I believe that He lived a sinless life and died on the cross for my sins. I believe that you resurrected Him from the dead on the third day. I believe and accept Jesus as my Savior. Please forgive me of my sins and make me born again. I repent of my sins and ask You to help me to serve You as my Lord and Savior. Please fill me with Your Holy Spirit. In Jesus Name I pray. Amen!"

Disclaimer Notice!

The words and definitions in the book and glossary are paraphrased and designed for being helpful in understanding the information in this book. These are not the Webster's Dictionary or formal definitions of these words. These words and definitions are formed to help you understand the ideas and information the author is trying to convey to you for Spiritual purposes. At no point in time is the author to be liable for a misrepresentation or improper understanding of these words and their described definition. Please consult the Bible for a proper understanding of any word you are trying to understand for Christian spiritual purposes. The example Sinner's Prayer can be used for leading someone to Christ. Use it as often as you need to for teaching or leading someone to Christ.

Breaking the Contract of Wrath

Answer these on a separate piece of paper

1. Who offended you?
2. What did they do to offend you?
3. List the next offense they did to you?
4. Keep listing the offenses until you can't think of anymore.
5. Why haven't you forgiven them in the past?
6. Why won't you forgive them now?
7. What if they died tomorrow?
8. Would you be mad at them beyond the grave? Why or why not?

Ephesians 4:32, "*And be kind to one another, tenderhearted, forgiving one another, even as God in Christ forgave you.*"

Mark 11:25, "*And whenever you stand praying, if you have anything against anyone, forgive him, that your Father in heaven may also forgive you your trespasses.*"

"Lord I forgive _____ for sinning against me. I need Your Forgiveness Lord. I am trapped by the Contract of Wrath. I release them for all that the enemy did through them. They sinned against me on purpose but I forgive them for what they did. Even if they are not sorry for what they did I still forgive them and release them. I forsake my plans for revenge. Lord help me to pray for this person daily and show them the Love of God. Help me to walk in Love and to be filled with Your Love. In Jesus Name I pray Amen."

<u>Breaking the Contract of Fear</u>

Answer these on a separate piece of paper

1) What is a Biblical definition of fear?
2) Why do you fear?
3) Make a list of the things that you fear.
4) When did you first start to fear? Why?
5) What happened to make you fear?
6) What does the Bible say about Fear (See Chapter 10)?
7) What has God told you about fear?
8) Why are you disobeying God and choosing to fear?
9) Why not just trust in God instead of choosing to be in fear?
10) Why are there 365 verses in the Bible about fear?
11) What Spirit did God give us? (2 Timothy 1:7)
12) Does fear solve the problem? (Matthew 6:33-34)
13) Are you tired of dealing with fear? Do you want to be free?

"Lord I come to You today and I want to be free from fear. I want to break the Contract of Fear. I see that fear is not Biblical and it is demonic. I give you all of my fears, doubts, worries, and concerns. The Bible says to trust You and not lean on my own understanding. Lord I release my logical mindset and choose not to fear. I rebuke the spirit of fear! Leave my life. I renounce all thoughts and any devotions I have to the spirit of fear. My identity is hidden in Jesus Christ. Father I trust You with my life. I surrender my plans for my life to You. Help me to trust You with all of my heart. I believe that no weapon formed against me will prosper! In Jesus Name I pray. Amen!"

Breaking the Contract of Pride

Answer these on a separate piece of paper

1) Do you think you are smarter than God sometimes?
2) Do you fully obey the Word of God every day?
3) Do you judge others for their actions?
4) Do you think you have learned all you can from the Bible?
5) Do you go days without praying and spending quality time with God?
6) Do you think your perception is the only right one?
7) Do you find it difficult to forgive people sometimes?
8) Do you think you have mastered the Christian Religion?
9) Do you think you are close to perfect most of the time?

If you answered yes to any of these questions then you have been prideful. Pride is hard to recognize sometimes but the Holy Spirit will speak to you about it if you are humble and willing to listen. We have to repent from all areas of pride in our lives. This takes humility and realizing that we are nothing but dust. We are not to think of ourselves as more important than others. We cannot think that we can disobey God's Word and it is ok. Read Scriptures on pride and destroy the power it has over your life. Let's pray and Break the Contract of Pride. Proverbs 3:7 says, *"Do not be wise in your own eyes; Fear the LORD and depart from evil."*

"Heavenly Father I ask that You would forgive me of my arrogance and pride. I am foolish to think that I am above following Your Word. I have been living a lie and I ask You to please forgive me of my sins. I am prideful and ask for Your Forgiveness. Help me to be humble and to be a servant. Help me to put others first, help them, and not judge them. I am grateful for Your Grace. Help me to show Love, Mercy, and Grace to everyone I encounter. I Break the Contract of Pride in my life. Help me to honor, respect, and follow Your Precious Word. In Jesus Name I pray. Amen!"

Breaking the Contract of Worldliness

Answer these of a separate piece of paper

1) What is worldliness according to the Bible (See Chapter 10)?
2) Are you in a sin pattern that you can't seem to break?
3) Do you believe that you are a worldly Christian?
4) Do you think it is ok to not obey some parts of the Bible?
5) Do you fully obey the Word of God?
6) Do you pray and read your Bible every day?
7) Do you go to Church faithfully?
8) Are you involved in sharing your faith about Jesus to others?
9) Are you passionate about the Presence of God and being with Him?

If you answered yes to questions 2-4 or no to questions 5-9 then you are being a worldly Christian and have signed a Contract of Worldliness with the enemy. The enemy is keeping you from being effective for God and you must repent.

"Heavenly Father I realize that I have been a worldly Christian. I have been convicted of these sins but have never fully repented. I have accepted the lie that You are ok with me being a lukewarm Christian. I ask that You would forgive me for being rebellious and selfish. Help me to get on fire for You and to put You first in everything that I do. Please forgive me for all of my sins! I need You in my life. I repent and ask You to help me to put Your Will above my own. I am tired of not pleasing You and being in rebellion to the Great Commission. I am sorry and I pray that You will help me to get in Church and serve You with all of my heart, soul, mind, and strength! In Jesus Name I pray Amen!"

Made in the USA
Middletown, DE
30 December 2021

57243963R00104